Chess Opening Names

The Fascinating & Entertaining History Behind The First Few Moves

Nathan Rose

Foreword by GM Simon Williams

© Stonepine Publishing

First Edition, 2017

ISBN: 978-0-473-39673-2

Table of Contents

Bonus Content

This book's companion website is www.chessopeningnames.com. Once you have learned the story behind the chess opening names, you can learn how to master playing them via the professionally-produced video training courses on offer.

There are several free bonuses for readers of *Chess Opening Names* to download:

- A pgn file of all the openings and variations named in this book, so you can play through and practice them on your computer.
- A family tree index of all the moves named in this book – for example, which moves are branches of the "core" openings, and the points at which the different names diverge.
- A video explanation of how algebraic chess notation works – helpful for those who are not yet familiar with the meaning of script such as **1. e4 e5**, which is used throughout this book.
- Sample chapters of my other books.

To download these free bonuses, head to www.chessopeningnames.com, scroll to the "Bonus Content" section and use your email address to subscribe.

The website is also where I invite readers to share their feedback on *Chess Opening Names*. Please feel free to request the stories behind more names that didn't make it into this edition! If a name is requested frequently, I will add it to the website and to future editions of the book. Email subscribers will be the first to know about new opening names as they are added.

Foreword: GM Simon Williams

The wife is fed up.

For many nights now, her husband has locked himself, alone, in his home office. One night, tiptoeing to the door, she overhears a cryptic phone conversation; *"I tried a Slav last weekend, but it was rather unexciting. Next time I'll go for a Scandinavian! Yes… queen takes d5 is the way I may continue…"*.

Such language is foreign to her. What illicit activities is he concealing? The wife grows increasingly suspicious as her partner locks himself away more frequently, returns home late on weeknights looking stressed or upbeat, and takes more and more "work-related" trips on weekends with his phone switched off for several hours at a time.

Enough is enough. The wife makes the necessary arrangements to track her husband's movements and catch him in the act once and for all. She discovers he is visiting the same location on a regular basis – a mid-priced hotel in a far-flung town.

She decides it is time to confirm her worst fears. As he sets off on one of his Friday-to-Sunday "business trips", she stealthily follows behind under the cover of the evening darkness. Bursting into the hotel, she finds her husband, prone, deep in concentration. *"It's worse than I could possibly have imagined!"*, she exclaims incredulously, *"He has taken up chess!"*.

Though the above story is a work of fiction, the underlying theme is not unknown to chess players and their non-chess playing partners. Those who are not familiar with the game are bemused by the intricate language the chess enthusiast adopts. The *"Fried Liver Attack"* sounds like something out of a B-rated horror film. Statements such as *"I got myself tied up in a Maróczy Bind"* are downright strange to the novice of chess, but become second nature to the developing player. By employing a specialist lexicon, chess players feel part of a secret society. It transcends ordinary barriers and unites players worldwide, regardless of their native language.

Many of these special code names are found within the chess player's constant obsession: opening theory. This is not the first book to be written on chess openings, and it won't be the last. In fact, chess publishing is absolutely dominated by it; hundreds of books are published each year; countless papers, diagrams and games are devoted to just one variation of one opening!

It would be impossible to know all the variations to

all the chess openings; after just five moves, there are more possibilities than grains of sand in the sea. But all players must have wondered, as they are studying and preparing, where did all these names come from? "Alekhine's Defense" is not the Alekhine's Defense for nothing! Isn't the "Giuoco Piano" a classical instrument? Is the "Grand Prix Attack" covertly sponsored by Formula 1?

This book answers these questions and many more. It is a new and unique look at the chess openings from an informative and historical perspective, accessible to the chess-obsessed and non-chess players alike. Rather than bore the reader with deep technical analysis, Nathan Rose aims to explain the origin of the nomenclature of many common openings and variations; introducing the fascinating personalities, locations and tales behind their invention and development. All this is done in a manner which is well-defined, structured and, most importantly, fun. After all, fun is the main reason we play chess!

I'm certain that all readers, new and seasoned, young and old, will enjoy this overview on the origins of chess opening names. It is not the best kept secret that I progressed from club player to master based on my nightly readings of tactics books from the comfort of my bath. Had it been published, I'm sure that this book would have been high on my reading list!

On a personal note, whether you are new to chess, or a knowledgeable (and now slightly worn out and despondent) grandmaster, I would like to remind readers that chess is a wonderful game which can enrich your life in so many ways. It has allowed me to travel the world while meeting and playing other like-minded people.

During my chess career, I have been fortunate to make the acquaintance of some of the most interesting characters in society; the slightly nerdy accountant-types, the eccentrics, the egomaniacs, the young whippersnappers, the mad geniuses. All have been bitten by the chess bug – and once you are bitten, there is no cure!

The beauty of chess is it can be whatever you want it to be. It transcends language, age, race, religion, politics, gender and socioeconomic background. Whatever your circumstances, anyone can enjoy a good fight to the death over the chess board.

It is important to have a creative pursuit; whether that be making or enjoying music, the visual feast of an art gallery or knitting tiny hats for cats! My art is created on a 64-square board, and it has brought an immeasurable amount of pleasure to my life.

"Chess doesn't drive people mad, it keeps mad people sane." - **Bill Hartston**

Grandmaster Simon Williams

www.gingergm.com

Introduction

Why do people play chess?

Many complex theories have been advanced to explain the game's enduring popularity, but I have a very simple one: <u>humans like to prove how clever they are to each other.</u> Winning at chess is one way to prove yourself as superior, but it is far from the only way. For example, an extensive knowledge of history will do the job every bit as effectively.

Imagine leaning back in your chair and telling your opponent that you were tempted to play the "Berlin Defense" against his "Ruy López", but decided to play "Morphy's Defense" instead. Then you can ever-so casually enquire "You do know why these openings are named that, don't you?" Then you can explain everything to your ignorant adversary and bask in their jealous admiration. That way, even if your opponent beats you over the chess board, you will still hold the intellectual ascendancy.

The tales behind chess opening names are less well-known than the moves themselves. This is a pity. The origins of the names are richly intertwined with world history, the enthralling lives of the great grandmasters of the past, and the critical contests which have shaped chess through the centuries. These fascinating and entertaining stories are about to be revealed to you.

One thing this book won't do is improve your chess playing strength. If you want a comprehensive guide to opening play, you can take your pick from literally thousands of other tomes, journals and guides. But let's face it, to the casual player (and indeed, to many club players), most other chess books are mind-numbingly boring.

Learning chess openings is a particularly excruciating exercise in rote memorization: move this pawn here, then if your opponent moves his pawn there, then move your knight over here, but if your opponent instead moves his bishop, then move your queen. Repeat for hundreds of pages. You lose interest in the book. Tragically, you might even lose interest in chess altogether.

Even if, against all odds, you grit your teeth and finish these books, you will likely forget what you are supposed to do when you face up to a real, human opponent and don't have the book to refer to. Or worse, your opponent could do something which your book didn't even cover.

Such opening study is unavoidable for those who

want to reach the highest echelons of chess, but for the rest of us, chess is more of a hobby. Hobbies are meant to be enjoyed, not endured. This book will help with something even more important than playing better chess – how to appreciate the game more.

Sport is meaningless without knowing the players, the history and the rivalries. If we aren't emotionally invested in the outcome, it's just people in brightly colored uniforms kicking a ball around. To rouse our interest, we must have context to the stories behind the game and understand why they matter. In the same vein, you will get a lot more pleasure out of chess if you understand more about its past. That is exactly what this book will help you do. It will burrow down rabbit holes and go off on tangents. Additionally, expect a dose of comic relief from time to time – many people take chess much too seriously, so a little levity cannot hurt.

At the outset, it is important to emphasize that *Chess Opening Names* is primarily concerned with the <u>names</u>, and the life and times of the person, place, or story behind each name in question. Some names are shared between several moves: for instance, there is a "Steinitz Variation" in the Ruy López, Caro-Kann Defense, Sicilian Defense, Scotch Opening, Vienna Game, and the French Defense. If openings or variations share the same name, they will not be given separate treatment in this book. It would quickly become repetitive to tell and retell the story of a name for each variation, so this book uses one opening or variation to explain each unique name.

I will also be the first to admit that this book is not an encyclopedia of every opening or variation. *Chess Opening Names* is meant to be a light, easy read, and with literally thousands of named openings to choose from, not all could make the final cut. Some were obvious inclusions, the very obscure ones were easy to leave out, but there were also several on the edge between "in" and "out". Inevitably, some names fell on one side of the fence, and some on the other.

The overall criterion I used was to include an entry if the average club player or casual chess player is likely to have heard of it. Openings often made the cut if they involved just one or two moves (even if rare in actual play), but longer variations were also included if adjudged important enough. I resisted going beyond five moves into the game in all but one case. The result, I believe, is a book which covers all the main openings and variations, as well as a smattering of quirky less common ones.

I'll also quickly cover off a few openings here which were left out because the origin is plainly self-evident:

the "Queen's Gambit" is called that because it's a gambit on the queenside (and the "King's Gambit" is a gambit on the kingside). The "Four Knights Game" sees both players develop each of their knights, meaning four knights in total leave their starting squares. The "Bishop's Opening" features a bishop being developed by White on move two. There's really nothing more to say about the names of openings like these.

With that, let's commence our adventure through the eccentric people, captivating places and amazing stories which have given their names to the first few moves of chess.

The People

The chess players in this section are an eclectic collection of professors, clergy, drunks, visionaries and narcissists. You'll read about the noteworthy deeds they performed to leave their name indelibly upon an opening or variation, as well as something about the rest of their lives.

The reader may notice that some of chess's most significant figures are only mentioned in passing rather than having chapters of their own. In some cases, this is because they were not noted opening innovators; José Raúl Capablanca, Emanuel Lasker and Mikhail Tal fall into this camp. Others simply appeared too late – for instance, by the time Garry Kasparov rose to prominence in the 1980s, it was practically impossible to find novelties within the first few moves, because that shallow ground had already been picked over by players who had come before.

Most of the names in this section came about due to a player's use of the opening in high profile games, or through their contribution to the body of chess theory. The vast majority come from the 18th, 19th and early 20th centuries, the years when innovation in the first few moves was at its peak. The chapters are ordered roughly chronologically, based on the peak of the player's career. Additionally, an alphabetical index is located at the back of the book.

Ruy López

1. e4   e5
2. Nf3   Nc6
3. Bb5

Ruy López was a priest from Spain who lived all the way back in the 16th century. Some of the very oldest recorded games are attributed to López and his frequent sparring partner, Giovanni Leonardo Di Bona of Italy. Think of this, every time you sit down to play – through chess, you share a bond with those like López who lived hundreds of years ago. If you write your moves down, as yet unborn people will be able to replay your games long after you are gone and marvel at your brilliance (or lack thereof).

Apart from his duties as a man of God, López also wrote one of the first books about chess: *Libro de la invencion liberal y arte del juego del axedrez*. He penned it partly as a reply to an even earlier book, *Questo libro e da imparare giocare a scachi et de li partiti*, which Pedro Damiano of Portugal had written half a century prior. López apparently read *Questo* on a trip to Rome, disliked it, and resolved to write a better chess manual.

Libro contains some general strategic advice and a section on the historical origins of chess. It also includes the rules that were being used at the time, most of which are the same to this very day. Among the differences, *Libro* mentioned that a stalemate resulted in a win for the player not stalemated rather than a draw. A player could also win by capturing all his opponent's pieces, even if the enemy king remained un-checkmated. If you have known the frustration of completely outplaying your opponent, only to have the game end drawn, you might wish that we could bring these old rules back.

López's *Libro* is the reason we call the above sequence of moves the "Ruy López". *Questo* (Damiano's older book) argued that after **1. e4 e5, 2. Nf3**, Black's best next move was **2. ...Nc6**. López disagreed with Damiano, arguing that **3. Bb5** "refuted" **2. ...Nc6**. The claim was enough to affix López's name to the opening for evermore.

Today we know that **3. Bb5** is certainly not a refutation of **2. ...Nc6** and that the Ruy López opening is perfectly playable for Black. It is a strategically rich opening, and many other named variations are branches of the Ruy López.

Bear in mind, *Libro* was written over 400 years ago, and López was blazing the trail of opening theory. We stand on the shoulders of our ancestors, and if we improve upon what our they discovered, it shouldn't diminish their original achievement.

The Ruy López (also known as the "Spanish Opening") has been studied endlessly in the intervening centuries. You could spend months and years delving into the various lines which the sharpest minds in chess have pored over for all that time. Indeed, if you have any ambition to play chess at the top level, this is exactly the sort of intensive study that will be required. The Ruy López is one to avoid if you don't have much of an appetite for opening preparation, for you will quickly find yourself on the back foot if your opponent has crammed more theory into their head than you.

Later in life, Ruy López was elevated from the priesthood and became a bishop. A bishop of the religious kind, not the type found on a chess board – although the mental image of this pious Spaniard moving around the cobblestones of his town exclusively diagonally is certainly an amusing one.

Philidor Defense

1.	e4	e5
2.	Nf3	d6

François-André Danican Philidor came from a long line of extraordinary musicians – his grandfather, father, uncle, cousin and brother were all renowned performers, composers and concert organizers. The Philidor family played to French high society and the royal family for generations.

Philidor was born to a 72-year-old father and a 19-year-old mother (!). His father may have managed to sire a child to his teenage wife, but he didn't live to see his progeny grow beyond boyhood, dying when François-André was just four.

Following in the footsteps of his august forebears, Philidor became one of Europe's leading, and most prolific, opera composers. Such was his contribution, he is today honored with a bust of his likeness on the southwest façade of the Opéra Garnier in Paris. But while Philidor was unquestionably a renowned music composer, in chess he was truly without equal.

As a boy, Philidor was part of the royal choir. When he was 10 years old, Philidor suggested a game against a senior musician. Smirking, the man agreed, probably not expecting much of a contest from a child. But to his shock, the youngster won. Philidor ran off as soon as he checkmated his opponent, fearing the retribution of the man whose pride he had just wounded.

Philidor continued to improve from there. He received lessons from an older French great, Legall de Kermeur, and eventually surpassed him. He frequented the chess cafés of Paris, including the famed Café de la Régence, which you can read more about in this book's chapter on the Paris Opening. Philidor's chess reputation was cemented once he began touring Europe with his music. Wherever he went, he would arrange to face the city's strongest chess players. None could match him.

Despite his chess prowess, Philidor thought of himself as a musician first and foremost. Chess was only an amusement, not a vocation. Still, the game got him out of a tricky spot in 1745 when he was due to present 12 concerts in Rotterdam starring a girl who played the harpsichord. The girl died suddenly, the concerts were cancelled, and Philidor was left stranded, far from home and without money. He managed to pay his way back to Paris by teaching and playing chess.

Philidor also had a party trick up his sleeve – he could play chess blindfolded against several opponents at once. He got his opponents to sign affidavits of what he had done to provide evidence for (what he imagined would be) disbelieving future generations. Many have since replicated the feat, but at the time observers found blindfolded chess simuls to be utterly astonishing.

Being both a musical composer and a chess master made Philidor a model member of French intellectual life. He mingled in esteemed company, including several of the key writer/philosophers of the day. Philidor met and played against Benjamin Franklin, the businessman, inventor and statesman who later became one of the founding fathers of the United States of America. Franklin was a formidable chess player in his own right and enjoyed visiting Europe for the sterner test of his skills than he could hope for in the fledgling American colonies.

In 1749, Philidor published his book, *Analyse du jeu*

des Échecs. It was here that he recommended the little move **2. ...d6** for Black. Developing a second pawn to defend the first is a solid yet unspectacular way to play, but it was this same conservative style which made Philidor so notable.

One of the reasons Philidor kept winning was that he had a critical difference in opinion from virtually all his contemporaries when it came to pawns. Most players in the 18th century regarded pawns as rather irrelevant. They are the weakest soldiers at a player's command, and there are <u>eight</u> of them. Why not sacrifice one or two here or there if it helps to gain attacking momentum? But Philidor made the world realize the strength inherent in pawns, especially when they work together. Philidor said "Pawns are the soul of chess." Through his influence, players started treating their pawns with more care and consideration.

Philidor's musings about pawns came at around the same time as broader society was going through the Enlightenment: the idea that the common man was worthy of more than had been traditionally granted in a world dominated by monarchy, aristocracy and the church. Awareness was spreading largely thanks to the writings of many of Philidor's friends; among them Voltaire, Diderot, and Jean-Jacques Rousseau.

One can picture Philidor engaged in hushed, conspiratorial conversations concerning the parallels between the elite's disregard for the plebian classes and chess players' disregard for pawns.

The Enlightenment led to America's Declaration of Independence, the improvement of rights for the common man – and most significantly for Philidor, the French Revolution. His long service to the king, elevated position in society and privileged upbringing made him just the sort of bourgeoisie that was guillotined by the thousand during the French Reign of Terror.

Philidor was in England when the French Revolution struck. Unable to return to France, he lived out the rest of his days in London. His music found little appreciation there, so he had to eke out a meager existence from chess. He never saw his wife again, became depressed and died alone. A tragic end for such a talented man, but his music is still occasionally played, and so is his opening.

Evans Gambit

1.	e4	e5
2.	Nf3	Nc6
3.	Bc4	Bc5
4.	b4	

Chess has been referred to as "The Royal Game" thanks to the favor it historically gained with kings, courtiers and the landed gentry. In the 18th century and earlier, the nobility were the only ones who had enough excess money and free time that they could afford to lounge around and move little figurines around a 64-square board. The poor were understandably more concerned with mere survival and had no time for such frivolity.

This makes the Evans Gambit interesting, for it was not named after a member of the upper classes. While the family of the Welshman William Evans were sufficiently well-off to send their child to a grammar school, the lad had no life of idle leisure to look forward to. Evans became a sailor, and his early years saw him voyage off to distant ports in the West Indies and the Mediterranean Sea. Eventually he rose to be appointed captain of a Post Office steamship that made short, regular journeys back and forth between Milford Haven in Wales and Waterford in Ireland.

These routine crossings of St. George's Channel left Evans with plenty of downtime to study chess. One day, he came up with the startling **4. b4** move after the typically conservative Giuoco Piano (**3. ...Bc5**). If Black is expecting a quiet start to the game, then **4. b4** instantly shakes him from his slumber.

To the uninitiated, the Evans Gambit looks like an awful gaffe from a rank beginner; Black can simply capture the undefended pawn with **4. ...Bxb4**. But this is exactly White's plan – that pawn is sacrificed to gain rapid development. One continuation sees White play **5. c3**, forcing Black's bishop away to **5. ...Ba5**, and then White surges forward in the center with **6. d4**.

Position after 6. d4.

While on shore leave in London, Captain Evans played his gambit in a game against the leading British player of the early 19th century, Alexander McDonnell. McDonnell was checkmated in just 20 moves, leaving him stunned but also impressed by the novel opening that had just been used to beat him. When William Lewis, another influential British chess figure, later wrote an analysis of the move in a book of all known openings, he referred to it as "Evan's Gambit". Thus, the name was confirmed.

All of this was happening in the 1830s and 1840s, when chess was at last growing past society's old dividing lines. A middle class with better incomes and more leisure time was on the rise. No longer was chess exclusively "The Royal Game", and what's more, the masses could now play the Evans Gambit, an opening named after an ordinary sea captain.

Away from the chessboard, Evans also invented a naval lighting system which prevented collisions between ships at night. For this lifesaving discovery, he was awarded the then handsome sum of £1,500 by an appreciative British government and a further £200 and a gold chronometer from the Tsar of Russia. For his famous chess gambit, Evans was awarded nothing of monetary value, but he did get lasting fame, which is something that money can't buy.

Petrov's Defense

1.	e4	e5
2.	Nf3	Nf6

Alexander Petrov was the first great Russian chess master. It makes Petrov the father figure of a rather large extended family, given how many champions have come from Russia and the Soviet Union in the years since.

Chess can be played throughout an entire lifetime, a fact which can easily be verified by visiting a local club. There, you will meet pre-pubescent children whose arms are not yet long enough to reach the other side of the board. There will also be a fair number of old-timers – wrinkled, wheezing and half-deaf.

Petrov was further evidence of chess's ability to be a lifelong companion. He lived between 1794 and 1867, learning the game as a four-year-old, was the best player in Russia before he was 20, and remained dominant even as his old age granted him a set of imposing white whiskers. He was his country's strongest player for a full half century, which even by chess standards represents incredible longevity.

Petrov spent his life in Eastern Europe and only embarked on short trips to Vienna and Paris after he had finally retired from playing chess competitively. The tyranny of distance meant that games between Petrov and the Western European masters such as Alexander McDonnell, Pierre Charles Fournier de Saint-Amant and Howard Staunton never materialized. We'll simply never know where Petrov ranked among them.

In addition to being a fine player, Petrov was also a chess puzzle composer and an author. His 1824 book *Shakhmatnaya igra* wrote about **2. ...Nf6** as an option for Black. Large tracts of the rest of this book were copied from other authors, but the work on **2. ...Nf6** was original.

At first glance, Petrov's Defense seems to portend a tit-for-tat exchange of the e-pawns, but this apparent threat is a mirage. If White captures with **3. Nxe5**, and an inexperienced Black player automatically responds in kind with **3. ...Nxe4**, then **4. Qe2** sees White able to force an advantage. The natural-looking retreat of **4.**

...Nf6 compounds Black's woes, as **5. Nc6+** will win Black's queen on the spot.

Position after 5. Nc6+. Black's queen is lost.

Petrov's Defense has a reputation for being rather dull if it proceeds exactly according to opening theory. However, for casual players where deep knowledge of the theoretical lines is absent, things can quickly spring to life in Petrov's Defense if either side missteps.

Schliemann-Jaenisch Gambit

1.	e4	e5
2.	Nf3	Nc6
3.	Bb5	f5

This opening is variously called the "Jaenisch Gambit", the "Schliemann Defense", and the double-barrelled "Schliemann-Jaenisch Gambit" to credit both men.

Carl Jaenisch was by far the more significant player and was the first to play the opening at the top level, over a decade before Adolph Schliemann adopted the idea. Furthermore, when Schliemann was playing a Black pawn to f5 in the 1860s, he was doing so on move four, after first playing **3. ...Bc5**. Yet Schliemann, a lawyer by profession, still succeeded in getting his name associated with **3. ...f5**.

The Schliemann-Jaenisch Gambit will often upset White's rhythm. Many Ruy López players will not be at all familiar with it. One of the most common errors that the unprepared White player tends to make is to grab the offered pawn. Capturing looks natural, for playing a pawn to f5 resembles a reversed-color King's Gambit, where accepting the sacrifice is the norm. But in the Schliemann-Jaenisch Gambit, this is a mistake; after **4. exf5   e4**, theory opines that Black has either gained equality, or even a slight advantage. White's other potential fourth move replies also hide some demons, making the Schliemann-Jaenisch Gambit an enjoyable opening to turn to if you thrive in early complications.

Position after 4. ...e4.

Jaenisch was born in a town close to St. Petersburg. He began his career as an army engineer but left in order to devote himself more fully to chess. At around the same time, Jaenisch wrote a book, *Analyse*

Nouvelle des ouvertures (English: "A New Analysis of Chess Openings"), where he did the work on **3. ...f5**. It was translated to English in 1847 and the gambit came to be associated with him.

Chess players are often left-brained by nature, favoring process and calculation. True to this, Jaenisch became an associate professor of mechanics in his career outside of chess. Having dedicated his life to chess and mathematics, Jaenisch became determined to prove a link between them in his major life's work – a three-volume book: *Traité des applications de l'analyse mathématique au jeu des échecs* (English: "Treatise on the Application of Mathematical Analysis in the Chess Game").

Jaenisch was always just behind Alexander Petrov in the stakes of the best player in Russia. Petrov had, in fact, tutored Jaenisch, but the apprentice never quite surpassed the master. Still, Jaenisch was good enough to be invited to play at the famed London 1851 chess tournament (more on this event later), but failed to arrive in time.

Falkbeer Countergambit

1.	e4	e5
2.	f4	d5

Ernst Falkbeer lived his young adult years in Vienna. In those days, the Austrian Empire encompassed Germans, Slovenes, Czechs, Slovaks, Ukrainians, Croats, Italians, Serbs, Poles, Hungarians and Romanians – none of which shared a common language. Many were agitating for greater autonomy or even independence, culminating in the 1848 revolutions. The Austrian Empire had also restricted the freedom of the press, which affected Falkbeer more than most due to his occupation as a journalist.

Falkbeer fled to Germany and played a few matches with better known players such as Henry Bird and Johann Löwenthal, as well as being a frequent opponent of Adolf Anderssen. It was while playing Black against Anderssen in 1851 in response to the

King's Gambit (**2. f4**) that Falkbeer tried **2. ...d5**.

The "romantic era" of chess was in full swing in Falkbeer's time, characterized by swashbuckling combinations, sacrifices galore and chess as a form of artistic expression rather than technically correct play. The King's Gambit enjoyed immense popularity – a pawn is immediately offered in order to open lines for attack.

Back then, it was considered ungentlemanly to decline a gambit, a notion which seems quaint nowadays. But what did chivalry have to say about a countergambit? Yes, **2. ...d5** sees the King's Gambit declined, yet another gambit is offered in its place. **3. exd5** will often be followed by **3. ...c6**, inviting **4. dxc6 Nxc6**, a line which results in White being a pawn up and behind in development – exactly the opposite of what might have expected after starting with the King's Gambit.

Position after 4. ...Nxc6.

Gambit players are happiest when they are attacking and dictating terms. But after the play of a countergambit, the tables are turned; the original gambiteer is now on the back foot and often out of their comfort zone. The hunter has become the hunted.

Falkbeer was eventually able to return to Vienna and wrote for several chess publications for the rest of his life, as well as trying to start his own publication (although this only lasted a few months).

Staunton Gambit

1. d4   f5
2. e4

The proud and hugely influential Englishman Howard Staunton is a name that every chess aficionado ought to be familiar with. The United Kingdom and France have been rivals for centuries, and so too over the chess board. 1834 had seen the British Alexander McDonnell lose to Louis-Charles Mahé de La Bourdonnais of France over a long series of matches. Then in 1843 Staunton redeemed his nation's pride when he beat the Frenchman Pierre Charles Fournier de Saint-Amant in a match held at the Café de la Régence in Paris. This victory boosted Staunton's celebrity and meant that he was generally regarded as the world's strongest player. He became a leading commentator with a regular chess column in *The Illustrated London News*, and wrote his most famous work, *The Chess-Player's Handbook*.

Staunton gave his name to this gambit thanks to winning with it in 1846 against a highly regarded German master, Bernhard Horwitz. **2. e4** is a very sharp response to the Dutch Defense. Black is offered an undefended pawn, but it carries the unmistakable whiff of a piece of bait. Whenever a decent opponent offers a sacrifice like this, you had best be on your guard. Theory says Black can indeed capture the offered e4 pawn, but there will be plenty of work to do before getting to safety.

Staunton used his considerable profile to organize a chess tournament to coincide with the London Great Exhibition of 1851. The best players from around Europe were invited, the first time that leading masters had all congregated in one place to play. Before that, sporadic matches had been organized between two players at a time. The gathering saw 16 players participating in a four-round knock-out contest to find one winner.

Before the event, Staunton was regarded as the favorite to win, but he lost to Adolf Anderssen of Prussia 4-1 in the semi-finals. Worse still, Staunton was rather ungracious in the aftermath of his defeat. He called Anderssen the <u>second</u>-best player in Germany (a bit of an insult, given Anderssen had just won this international tournament). Staunton also blamed his own poor showing on having had too little time to prepare due to being the tournament organizer – perhaps true, but making excuses did Staunton's reputation no favors.

Staunton stopped playing competitive chess in the mid-1850s when he received a contract to edit Shakespearean plays. However, in 1858 he was urged out of retirement by the American Paul Morphy (of whom you will read much more about later). Morphy had bested all competition in the United States and desired a match against the old English master. First Morphy asked Staunton to travel to New Orleans, but this was impractical given Staunton's commitments to his Shakespeare work. Undeterred, Morphy offered to travel to Europe, and Staunton agreed to play provided he had enough time to get back into practice.

What happened next remains contentious. Morphy kept pressing for a date to play, but Staunton kept asking for delays. Critics of Staunton say he was leading Morphy on and had never intended to play, but on the other hand, there is evidence that Staunton damaged his health trying to fulfill his duties to the Shakespeare work while also getting his chess back up to scratch (he had suffered from serious heart palpitations earlier in his life). The upshot: the two never played, much to Morphy's annoyance, as the prospect of facing Staunton was one of the chief reasons he had traveled across the Atlantic in the first place.

Another of Staunton's contributions relates to the shape of the chess pieces that have become the international standard for tournament play. If you doubt the importance of standardization, try playing chess sometime with an ornamental set of unfamiliar designs. As lovely as these old chess sets are, difficulty in telling between a pawn, bishop and rook quickly becomes exasperating.

Nathaniel Cooke, the editor of *The Illustrated London News*, registered a patent for a style of chessmen in 1849 and, to help the design catch on, he asked Staunton to use his column to recommend and give his name to the set of pieces. Staunton was well-incentivized to do so, for he received a fee for each set sold. They became known as the "Staunton" design and his endorsement undoubtedly helped them gain popularity.

Ordinarily, there would be no problem with sponsorships of this kind. Staunton, however, had earlier condemned the pursuit of chess as a profession – a rather hypocritical position, as most of Staunton's own earnings came through chess. It is fitting that a double-edged opening like the Staunton Gambit bears Staunton's name, for he had a distinctly double-edged personality.

Anderssen's Opening

1. a3

Adolf Anderssen is a critical figure in chess history, but the opening that bears his name is as fringe as the location of that pawn on the edge of the board. Moving the a-pawn ahead a single square makes no claim for the center. White essentially throws away the first move advantage and invites Black to play as though the colors were reversed.

Anderssen was one of the 16 participants at the famous 1851 London knockout tournament. Anderssen upset Howard Staunton in the semi-finals and went on to triumph over one of Staunton's lesser-known countrymen in the final, thus emerging as the tournament's winner. This is the moment most chess historians consider to be the end of Staunton's reign as the world's preeminent player.

Anderssen's most famous game was a casual

encounter played against Lionel Kieseritzky that came to be known as "The Immortal Game". Played at Simpson's Divan in London, it saw Anderssen sacrifice a bishop, both his rooks, and finally his queen to deliver a stunning checkmate with his remaining three minor pieces. Although on the losing side, Kieseritzky knew that he had been part of something special and he published the game in his journal, *La Régence*, along with generous annotations.

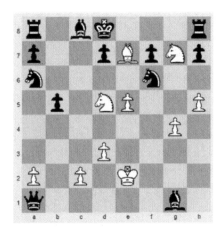

The Immortal Game checkmate. Anderssen was White.

In 1858, Paul Morphy crossed the Atlantic from America to challenge the great European masters. As Anderssen was now regarded as the best in Europe, he became the standard-bearer for the old world against this challenger from the new – all the more so because Howard Staunton didn't play Morphy at all.

By the time Anderssen faced Morphy, the American had developed a fearsome reputation. Morphy had already dispatched several formidable European players, so Anderssen was looking everywhere for an advantage ahead of their match. Perhaps an unexpected opening move to unsettle Morphy's preparation? Sure enough, Anderssen started with **1. a3** three times as White throughout their match. Morphy must have been taken aback by this strange move. Yet in these three games, Anderssen achieved an even 1 ½ points out of 3. Not bad, especially considering that over the entire match Anderssen was summarily crushed, losing seven, drawing two and winning two.

Having proven himself superior to all-comers, Morphy was now generally recognized as the strongest player in the world. But then, as you will read about in greater detail in Morphy's chapter, he went back to America and abandoned chess. With Morphy out of the picture, Anderssen again assumed the mantle of world's best until he lost a close match against Wilhelm Steinitz in 1866.

If you want to play Anderssen's Opening, rest assured that it will dumbfound your opponent. But psychological impact aside, if Black just plays to simple principles (develops pieces, controls the center, castles, and connects rooks), **1. a3** should not be troubling.

Morphy's Defense

1.	e4	e5
2.	Nf3	Nc6
3.	Bb5	a6

Paul Morphy is one of the most remarkable figures in chess history. During his brief career, he obliterated everyone he played, then vanished into the ether as suddenly as he had appeared.

Morphy was born into a privileged New Orleans family in 1837. As a young child, he learned chess by watching his father and uncle play on Sunday afternoons. His older relatives thought nothing of the child's interest in observing their games until one day, after the two older men had agreed to a draw, the boy shocked them by pointing out a complicated series of moves that both had missed which would have led to a win. The father and uncle didn't realize Paul even knew how the pieces moved, let alone such deep calculation.

It soon became clear the Morphy family had a child prodigy on their hands. The youngster had a photographic memory and an amazing intuitive feeling for the game. By the time he was 11, Morphy was already the best player in New Orleans. Aged just 12, he beat the visiting Hungarian professional Johann Löwenthal, three wins to zero.

3. ...a6 means that White's bishop cannot stay where it is. It must either retreat to a4, or capture the Black knight that it threatens. It is hardly a difficult move to spot in response to the Ruy López opening and countless players before Morphy would have played it. It appears that Morphy's Defense was named by accident, with Morphy himself only playing it a handful of times. One of these occasions was a Morphy-Löwenthal game recounted in William Cook's book *Synopsis of the Chess Openings*. In the fourth edition published in 1888, the book stated "Morphy's defense P-QR3 [or **3. ...a6** in modern notation] still holds good – but in modern practice there appears to be a tendency to defer playing it until learning the line of attack the first player proposes to adopt". Cook wrote "Morphy's defense" to refer to Morphy's singular game, but others started calling all Ruy López games which continued with **3. ...a6**

"Morphy's Defense" (with a capital "D").

When Morphy came of age, he went off to Spring Hill College to study the law. He was a bright student and finished his legal studies aged just 19 with the highest honors, but it was illegal for him to begin practicing as a lawyer professionally until he turned 21. To fill in his free time, Morphy turned back to chess and played at the First American Chess Congress in New York City in 1857. He was by far the youngest player in attendance, yet he swept all before him. Because of his moral conviction that chess should be an amateur game, Morphy refused all prize money.

Now recognized as the best player in America, Morphy's sights turned to the great chess masters of Europe. Where would he rank among this sterner competition? Most of all, Morphy wanted to play the legendary Englishman Howard Staunton. Staunton had been retired from chess for a few years, yet he agreed to play, so long as he had enough time to prepare. Morphy duly arrived in England, but Staunton kept requesting delays. Frustrated, Morphy gave up on Staunton and went to Paris instead. There, Morphy held many simultaneous and blindfold exhibitions at the Café de la Régence and played matches against Daniel Harrwitz and Adolf Anderssen, winning both convincingly. Anderssen even opined that Morphy was the strongest man ever to play the game.

Morphy's hometown of New Orleans is a former French colony and Morphy spoke French fluently. He rubbed shoulders with Parisian high society in between his chess games, though he became annoyed that chess was the only thing they wanted to talk about. Morphy felt there was more to him than just a chess player.

Having vanquished all serious opposition both at home and abroad, Morphy was widely acclaimed as the world's best. But, having apparently achieved all he wanted to in chess, Morphy decided to knuckle down and begin the serious business of establishing his law practice back home.

Unfortunately, Morphy was never able to ever make a success of being a lawyer. The outbreak of the American Civil War was a significant disruption, and even after the war Morphy's clients were more interested in discussing chess than their legal affairs. Morphy wanted to put chess firmly behind him, so it became exasperating when people kept bringing it up. By 1863 Morphy had become so negative about the game that he said, "I am more strongly confirmed than ever in the belief that the time devoted to chess is literally frittered away." He continually refused to use his chess prowess to make money, although he was approached countless times.

The Morphy family fortune meant that his failure to make it as a lawyer didn't leave him destitute, but his health still deteriorated. He moved back in with his mother and sister. He would talk to imaginary people, became convinced that conspiracies were working against him and died aged just 47.

Morphy made an amazing contribution to chess during his too-brief career, but this was overshadowed by the tragedy of him walking away from the game in his prime and subsequent early death. David Lawson's definitive biography of Morphy gave an apt summation of the man in the book's title: *The Pride and Sorrow of Chess.*

Caro-Kann Defense

1. e4   c6

The Caro-Kann Defense is named after two men: Horatio Caro of the United Kingdom and Marcus Kann from the Austro-Hungarian Empire. Neither were especially high profile, occupying that rung of the chess world just below the genuinely elite players.

Caro was born in England, but spent most of his career in Berlin. He was a regular in the Berlin city chess championship, winning it five times. His best individual wins were over Emanuel Lasker in 1890, and over Semyon Alapin in 1897.

Kann was from Vienna, and had his most famous victory when he beat Jacques Mieses in just 17 moves at the 1885 German Chess Congress while playing what is now called the Caro-Kann Defense. A year after that win, Caro and Kann worked together on developing the theory on the **1. ...c6** move, and co-published an article in a German magazine called *Brüderschaft*. Consequently, the opening became known as the Caro-Kann Defense.

The Caro-Kann Defense prepares Black for a d5 break with a supporting pawn. White's most common next move is **2. d4**, which Black will usually reply to with **2. ...d5**.

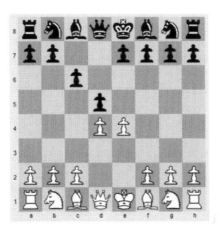

Position after 2. ...d5. The main line Caro-Kann Defense.

1. ...c6 was known about as far back as the 16th century, but never really caught on in the age of aggressive gambits and center occupation. It took decades after Caro and Kann's 1886 analysis for the best players to become advocates for the move. Black's light squared bishop is freer than in the French Defense, and Black can often get to an endgame with a better pawn structure. Respect has continued to grow, and these days it is a mainstay of many players' repertoires.

Bird's Opening

1. f4

Those new to chess will often be reluctant about moving their f-pawn early. The f2 square for White and the f7 square for Black represent the most salient vulnerability at the start of the game, defended only by the king. If an experienced player wants to score a cheap win over a beginner, it will often be through an early checkmate capturing or exploiting a weak f-pawn.

Bird's Opening violates the "don't move the f-pawn" principle on the very first move. Voluntarily throwing forward this key defensive stopper results in White's king being immediately exposed along the h4 to e1 diagonal. Playing such a move is the mark of a true fighter.

It may therefore surprise readers to learn that Henry Bird, the Englishman this double-edged opening is named after, was an accountant by trade – the dullest of all professions. Given the personality type typically associated with accountants (orderly, buttoned-down and conventional), it seems more appropriate for someone like him to be associated with a closed, slow opening.

One pictures Bird strolling to his local haunt in his dark suit and bowler hat after a long day of bean counting. He may have carried a drab leather briefcase filled with neatly summed ledgers. Finally, he gets to sit down, loosen his collar, and use chess to show off his repressed taste for danger. No messing around: he makes **1. f4** his first move and sits back in smug satisfaction as his opponent realizes all their opening preparation for a game starting with **1. e4** or **1. d4** has gone to waste. Game on.

In fact, it is quite common for someone's chess persona to be quite different from the rest of their character. Henry Bird is one example. Another is the Cuban José Raúl Capablanca (world champion between 1921 and 1927) – Capablanca lived the life of an international playboy, yet tended to play very pragmatically, belying his natural Latin American flair.

Bird participated in several strong European chess events held during the mid to late 19th century, including the famed 1851 London event, where he was knocked out in the first round. While Bird never won a major tournament, he did have occasion to play against other, more famous players including Paul Morphy and Wilhelm Steinitz.

Bird also wrote a few books about the game he loved, along with other books about railroad finance. He must have been a bit of a bore at parties. Try bringing up chess (or, I suppose, railroad finance) in casual conversation and the interaction will quickly fizzle, unless you chance upon a fellow enthusiast, in which case you will contentedly natter away about your shared obsession while everybody else makes a point of avoiding you.

The 15th century Spaniard Luis Ramírez de Lucena mentioned **1. f4** in his book *Repetición de Amores y Arte de Ajedrez*, (English: "Repetition of Love and the Art of Playing Chess") but it was Bird who had his name bestowed on the move, thanks to his profile in relatively more recent times. He first played it as a young man and continued to frequently trundle it out throughout his long career, leading the *Hereford Times* to name it in his honor in 1885.

Bird's Opening isn't often seen at master level due to certain weaknesses that can be exploited with correct play. But don't let that stop you from trying it as a surprise weapon. Amateur players don't play perfectly, and there is every chance you can spring a trap or two with Bird's Opening against an unprepared opponent.

Winawer Variation

1.	e4	e6
2.	d4	d5
3.	Nc3	Bb4

Szymon Winawer (pronounced "Veen-ah-ver" not "Win-a-wer") was a Jewish chess master from Warsaw, Poland. These days, grandmasters tend to reach their peak strength at a young age, but in Winawer's day they would often improve with age like a fine wine. His career at the top level spanned from a second-place finish in Paris in 1867, through to Monte Carlo in 1901 by which time he was 61 years old. In between, he won the first Polish chess tournament in 1868 and was also declared German chess champion in 1883.

In this variation of the French Defense, playing **3... Bb4** pins the knight and threatens a capture of White's e4 pawn. Often, Black will capture the c3 knight with his bishop, conceding the bishop pair to White, but White must pay the price of having doubled pawns on the c-file which Black can later target.

Sometimes an opening gets named for dubious reasons. The Winawer Variation is one such case. Although Winawer was known to play **3. ...Bb4**, he was neither the first to do so, nor the worthiest contributor to it. Plenty of others had tried the move before Winawer, and Aron Nimzowitsch was the one who really pioneered the deep theory on it decades later. The trouble is, Nimzowitsch already has another line in the French Defense named after him. It would be too confusing to name multiple variations within one opening system after Nimzowitsch, so Winawer got **3. ...Bb4** instead.

John Moles authored a book called *The French Defense: Main Line Winawer* in 1975. In it, Moles is scathing of Winawer's own ability to play the very opening that bears his name: "Even by the standards of his time he had little understanding of the problems of the defense... and while he himself presumably played the Winawer before 1867 it is unlikely that he even deserves to be considered an innovator." Ouch.

Albin Countergambit

1.	d4	d5
2.	c4	e5

Adolf Albin was born into a wealthy family of German descent in Romania. He moved to Vienna to study, and there learned chess at the advanced age of 20. These days, it would be impossible for a player to come to chess for the first time so late in life and still rise to the highest level. Modern players with serious aspirations of becoming a super-grandmaster need to be studying for hours a day before they even reach their teenage years. Yes, it robs them of a more "normal" childhood, but to succeed at the top level, this is what it takes. A youth with a more balanced upbringing simply will not have a chance against their more single-minded peers.

It took Albin until his 40s to become good enough to be invited to international tournaments. Although he would win a game here and there against the genuine greats, Albin was never close to reaching the zenith of chess.

The Albin Countergambit gained its name through a game of Albin's at an 1893 tournament in New York against Emanuel Lasker, who would win the world championship one year later. **2. ...e5** in reply to the Queen's Gambit was not totally unknown, but this was the first time it had been tried at such a high level. Playing White, Lasker still won the game, but **2. ...e5** gained the interest of analysts. Albin ended the tournament in second (behind Lasker), his best ever tournament result.

After the usual **3. dxe5   d4**, Black has a central outpost with his pawn on d4. A notable trap exists in this position, named after Albin's opponent in the same game – the "Lasker Trap". If it plays out, Black's d-pawn can march all the way down to promote on g1... but crucially, not promoting to a queen but to a knight!

4. e3	Bb4+
5. Bd2	dxe3
6. Bxb4	exf2+
7. Ke2	fxg1 = N+

The Lasker Trap. Position after 7. ... fxg1 = N+

Black has a huge advantage in this position. The knight cannot be captured due to the threat of **8. ... Bg4+.** The White king cannot move too far out of the way (say to e3 or f2), lest **8. ... Qxd1**, resulting in Black being a queen up. The best move for White is **8. Ke1**, but even this is met by the crushing **8. ... Qh4+.** Underpromoting to a knight (except as a joke in an already-won game) is the sort of move you might only get to make once in your lifetime, so make sure you are ready if and when the opportunity arises.

Albin's life took several fascinating twists. His family suffered political persecution. He ran a printing house, wrote the first ever chess book in Romanian, and worked as a translator for a railroad tycoon. He lost his entire fortune in stock market speculation and lived in America for a time. Given both his unconventional life and unconventional opening, perhaps it was Albin himself who summarized both most satisfactorily: "I chose to follow my own path into a variation which was regarded as wrong by the theory."

Steinitz Variation

1.	e4	e5
2.	Nf3	Nc6
3.	Bb5	d6

Wilhelm Steinitz was a near-sighted, portly man with a disproportionately large head. He leaned over the board and peered at the pieces and was barely five feet tall. But don't let his unimpressive physique fool you – Steinitz not only dominated chess, he transformed it. He was one of the game's deepest thinkers, and was such a seminal figure that there are over a dozen opening variations that bear his name.

When Steinitz began his career, the "romantic" era of chess was in full swing. Back then, the prevalent attitude was to attack the opponent's king aggressively and rapidly, often involving speculative sacrifices. Steinitz started his career in this vein too, but all that changed at an 1873 tournament in Vienna.

There, he unveiled a new way of playing, which came to be known as the "scientific" or "positional" style. His new plan involved avoiding permanent positional weaknesses and accumulating gradual advantages. If an opponent came at Steinitz with one of the usual onslaughts, he would sit back and deflect it, like a judo master who uses an assailant's own force against them.

Steinitz's key contention was that White and Black start the game equal and that perfect play by both sides should result in a draw. A win should thus be the reward for the player who makes the fewest mistakes. Therefore, Steinitz preached patience rather than slashing one's way to victory. This new philosophy immediately gained results for him. Starting at that Vienna tournament, he went on a 25-game winning streak against the world's other leading players.

Although successful, this way of playing made Steinitz very unpopular. Just imagine you were sitting inside one of the old chess coffee houses of the romantic era. Smoke and laughter fill the room. The chess is inspired. There are sacrifices aplenty, coins are being thrown to commend surprise checkmates, and everyone is having a rollicking good time. Then in walks Steinitz – that obstinate, ponderous fellow who spoils everyone's fun with drawn out prophylaxis. Groan.

Steinitz was declared the first universally recognized world chess champion by defeating Johannes Zukertort in 1886, but was widely regarded as the best player on the planet a full 20 years earlier. He beat Adolf Anderssen in a match in 1866, and was undefeated in match play from then until 1894 – an incredible 28 year reign.

Others assailed Steinitz's style as "cowardly". He vigorously defended his ideas through his column in *The Field* magazine and in the *International Chess Magazine* (which he founded and edited for many years). He was also a prolific commentator on the games of others. It is here, in these extensive writings, that the various openings named after Steinitz originate, including this variation of the Ruy López.

By the latter part of Steinitz's career, the sheer weight of results meant that the chess world could no longer credibly argue. The choice seemed to be: either learn how to play like Steinitz, or to keep losing to those who did. This was no choice at all for players whose earnings and livelihoods depended on winning. The romantic era of chess was over.

He survived three more world championship

challenges: two from Mikhail Chigorin from the Russian Empire, and one from Isidor Gunsberg from Austria-Hungary. Finally, in 1894, Steinitz's crown was taken by Emanuel Lasker of Germany. Three years later, they faced off again in a rematch, but by now Steinitz was quite elderly and well past his prime, and was easily defeated by the man 32 years his junior.

Chigorin Defense

1.	d4	d5
2.	c4	Nc6

When Mikhail Chigorin first saw chess, he didn't think much of it. But he decided it was worth another look when he finished his studies and began working for the government. He began to play at St. Petersburg's Café Dominik in his spare time and became so besotted with the game that he gave up his respectable job to pursue chess as a vocation.

Chigorin was widely regarded as the best player in Russia in the 1880s and 1890s. After a string of impressive tournament results, he challenged Wilhelm Steinitz for the world championship. His first attempt in 1889 saw Chigorin comfortably beaten by the incumbent.

The contest was much closer in the 1892 rematch. Chigorin found himself narrowly behind eight wins to nine in the first-to-10-win contest and had a golden opportunity to level the scores in game 23. He was ahead by a knight and had a completely winning endgame to look forward to. No one would have been at all surprised if Steinitz had resigned, such was the hopelessness of his situation. But in a stunning oversight, Chigorin moved the bishop holding his whole position together, gifting his opponent an obvious two-move checkmate. And just like that, Steinitz had won the match.

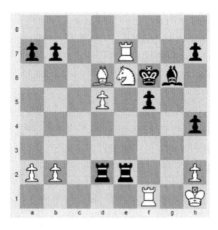

Chigorin (playing White) played 32. Bb4 here, allowing checkmate. 32. ...Rxh2+ 33. Kg1 Rdg2++

Every chess player knows the despair of working hard to earn a winning position only to throw it all away due to their own carelessness. It happens to all of us and mistakes are part of what makes us human. But tragically for Chigorin, his most egregious blunder happened at the worst possible time. It wasn't the sort of error that builds strength for having learned from it, it was the kind that one never recovers from and permanently stains a reputation. Even today, well over 100 years after the move was placed on the board, one can hardly mention Chigorin without reference to it.

Why do we blunder? Deep calculation requires us to block everything else from our minds, at times including what we already know. But in Chigorin's case, the swigs the burly man took from the bottle of brandy by his side may have had just as much to do with it.

The Chigorin Defense was introduced later in Chigorin's career at an 1895-96 tournament in St. Petersburg. Chigorin played **2. ...Nc6** in response to the Queen's Gambit, much to the surprise of his American opponent Harry Pillsbury – it was an unusual move back then, and it remains so today. However, Pillsbury recovered from his shock and defeated Chigorin. Later in the same tournament, another game took place between the two. Again, Chigorin was playing Black, and again he went with **2. ...Nc6**, but this time Chigorin emerged triumphant.

Chigorin was known as the last of a dying breed of gambit players. While everyone around him was switching to the positional style of Steinitz, Chigorin stuck fast to his tactical, imaginative roots. A 1903 tournament held in Vienna required everyone to play the King's Gambit, and Chigorin won, handily.

Chigorin also contributed greatly to the development of chess in Russia. He founded a club in St. Petersburg, traveled around the country to teach the game, and wrote columns for several magazines. He is regarded by many as the inspiration for the Soviet school of chess, which came to dominate the game in the second half of the 20th century. But for all his study, for all his tournament wins, for all else he did, Chigorin is famous primarily for that one crucial mistake in 1892. Oh, chess can be a cruel mistress.

Alapin's Opening

1. e4   e5
2. Ne2

Aside from chess, Semyon Alapin was also a skilled linguist, a railway engineer, and a grain merchant. He regularly entered international tournaments in the late 19th and early 20th century and was involved in many games against the more famous masters. Alapin's name will tend to feature (as an opponent) in any book about the heavyweights of the era, but he was never quite world championship material himself. At his peak, Alapin might have been around the world's 10th best chess player.

Aside from winning the world championship, an alternative way to gain chess fame is to do what Alapin did, and write. Alapin composed many chess puzzles and contributed greatly to the canon of opening theory. One of the amusing features of his analyses were the games he invented between two fictitious sparring partners with mirthfully Russian-sounding names: *Attakinsky* with the White pieces and *Defendarov* playing Black.

Study of chess openings will reveal "Alapin" variations sprinkled throughout. One of the best-known is the Alapin Variation of the Sicilian Defense, where White plays a pawn to c3 early in the game. You will see far more Alapin Sicilians than Alapin Openings in your lifetime, but from a purely egotistical point of view, it is surely preferable to have an entire opening named after you, rather than just a variation.

True, Alapin's Opening is a bit off-beat. *Batsford's Modern Chess Openings* renders no commentary other than the sneering "**2. Ne2** is a curiosity from a century ago", but this seems a bit harsh. Yes, that knight is awkward where it is, blocking both the queen and the bishop, but it can support a pawn break to f4, or find a home on g3. Additionally, it can be a tool to avoid heavily theoretical preparation by your opponent, given so many have dismissed Alapin's Opening.

Alapin rather starkly demonstrated the dangers of over-memorizing, through a game he played as Black against Siegbert Tarrasch in 1889. Things started calmly enough:

1.	e4	e5
2.	Nf3	Nf6

It had started as a Petrov's Defense. Alapin hailed from Vilnius (in modern day Lithuania), which at the time was part of the Russian Empire. In his youth, Alapin had moved the short distance north to study at the Engineering Institute in St. Petersburg, the city Petrov himself had called home. Therefore, we can safely assume Alapin was very familiar with the opening – too familiar, as we will see. The game continued:

3.	Nxe5	d6
4.	Nf3	Nxe4

All normal so far. Next move, Tarrasch pushed his d-pawn. Alapin picked up his bishop in reply, as he had done so many times before, but was suddenly hit by a sinking feeling. White's pawn had been played <u>one</u> square forward, not the more normal two squares! Tarrasch had threatened Alapin's knight with **5. d3** and Alapin had just left it hanging there.

Position after 5. d3. Next move, Alapin (playing Black) didn't move the knight on e4 out of the way.

Tarrasch grabbed the knight and Alapin immediately resigned. He must have felt as red-faced as a giant matchstick. Even if you don't adopt his opening, remember this parting lesson from Alapin: look at the board and respond to what your opponent does, not merely to what you expected them to do.

Maróczy Bind

1. e4   c5
2. Nf3   Nc6
3. d4   cxd4
4. Nxd4 g6
5. c4

Géza Maróczy (pronounced "Maro-zee") was a Hungarian master who reached his peak strength in the late 19th and early 20th century, performing well enough in tournaments to become a potential challenger to Emanuel Lasker's world championship title. A match was in fact agreed for 1906, but political problems in Cuba (the host country) scuttled the endeavor and Maróczy never got another chance.

Maróczy had a defensive style, perhaps a manifestation of his career as an engineer. When designing structures, the most important thing is to make sure they don't collapse. The chess version of such an attitude will be to pursue a similar "safety first" approach.

Maróczy was described as a kindly, self-effacing gentleman, but he was not completely above a bit of one-upmanship. In the late 1920s, Maróczy had been retired from international play for around 20 years and was in his 60s. A brash new generation of Hungarians were saying Maróczy was past his prime, so he decided to put the youngsters in their place.

According to an account from José Raúl Capablanca, Maróczy said, "These young Hungarian players are nothing special. They play well but are at most players of the second or third rank. They do not know the real game the great masters play; but they believe they know a great deal and they say they are stronger than I. For my part I am now old, I do not have the same interest as before, but their claims have annoyed me so much that I have told them I am ready to play a match with any of them." A match was duly arranged between Maróczy and Géza Nagy, who had recently won the Hungarian national championship. Maróczy thrashed the younger man five wins to zero.

The Maróczy Bind was known for years as a neutralizing tactic for White to employ against the Sicilian Defense. It is not an opening per se, but a setup – many positions arising from the Sicilian that feature White pawns on c4 and e4 and Black's c-pawn being exchanged for White's d-pawn are also given the name. The idea is to make it difficult for Black to play d5, a move which would free his cramped position. Later in the 20th century it became more acceptable for Black to enter the Maróczy Bind willingly. Playing the setup as Black is what Maróczy himself would sometimes do.

The most bizarre story about Maróczy came decades after his death. According to followers of the paranormal, the Soviet-born grandmaster Viktor Korchnoi played a game against Maróczy's ghost. A Swiss stockbroker arranged for Maróczy to communicate his moves via a man who didn't even know how to play chess, Robert Rollans. With Maróczy allegedly communicating from the ethereal plane, Rollans played out an expert-level game in a style very much reminiscent of Maróczy.

People are understandably skeptical about the story's veracity, but if you believe it, Korchnoi won in 47 moves. This would represent a more than respectable result for Maróczy against an elite grandmaster who had all the benefit of several extra decades of advancements in chess opening theory and strategy... especially considering Maróczy also had the distinct handicap of having no heartbeat.

Tarrasch Defense

1.	d4	d5
2.	c4	e6
3.	Nc3	c5

Siegbert Tarrasch of Germany was as influential as any of his contemporaries of the late 19th and early 20th century. He was a very clever man; as well as being one of the era's strongest chess players, he maintained a successful medical practice at the same time.

Tarrasch did, however, have a regrettable habit of rubbing people up the wrong way. He wore a pair of serious spectacles in front of his stern glare – the visage of a man who is extremely sure of himself and his opinions. It is easy to imagine him unleashing the full force of his intellect on anyone who dared disagree.

In many respects, Tarrasch's chess style resembled

that of Wilhelm Steinitz. Like the first world champion, Tarrasch favored control of the center and using "correct" play to accumulate small advantages to convert into an eventual win. He was a natural candidate to challenge Steinitz for the world championship and was even offered the opportunity to do so in 1892, but declined due to his commitments as a doctor.

Tarrasch also wrote books on chess. His 1912 book *Die moderne Schachpartie* (English: The Modern Chess Game) recommended **3. ...c5** as a way of declining the Queen's Gambit. As a leading player, his name became associated with the variation. Other masters felt it was dubious, as it leaves Black with a weak, isolated queen's pawn after **4. cxd5   exd5,** but Tarrasch argued that the mobility gained for Black makes up for it.

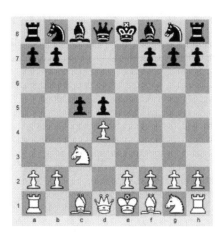

Position after 4. ...exd5.

In his analysis of other players' games, Tarrasch made a point of giving **3. ...c5** an exclamation mark in the notes, denoting a brilliant move. Of course, to Tarrasch it <u>was</u> brilliant – it was his idea! And to drive home the point, <u>any</u> other move would earn a question mark from the good doctor, the indication of a clear blunder.

Tarrasch had his chance to challenge for the world crown when he and Emanuel Lasker clashed in 1908. They didn't get on very well – when they were introduced to one another ahead of the contest, Tarrasch had this to say: "To you, Dr. Lasker, I have only three words: check and mate". Charming. But Lasker had the last laugh, handily defeating Tarrasch eight wins to three.

Aside from his world championship attempt, the central role Tarrasch occupies in chess history is that of the chief critic of the "hypermodern" school. The hypermodern players defied the dogmas laid down by men like Tarrasch and Steinitz. They advocated flank openings which sought to control the center from the sides, rather than occupying it with pawns.

Tarrasch was scathing in his reproach of those espousing these ideas which so fundamentally challenged his own. The rivalry he shared with Aron Nimzowitsch is especially legendary. While the elite level of chess is filled with gigantic egos, none quite match Tarrasch-Nimzowitsch for the level of venom displayed. Tarrasch represented the old guard that Nimzowitsch and the rest railed against, and this made them natural adversaries.

Their vehement philosophical disagreement was topped off with a generous helping of personal dislike. Tarrasch said of Nimzowitsch: "He alone has a preference for strange, bizarre, even hideous moves in the opening with which he has been lucky from time to time." Nimzowitsch didn't mince his words either: "Tarrasch, to me, always meant mediocrity; it is true that he was a very strong player, but all his views, his sympathies and antipathies, and above all his inability to conceive any new idea – all this clearly attested to the full mediocrity of his cast of mind."

Because of the contempt the two men shared for each other, their meetings over the chess board carried an extra bite. The 1914 game between Tarrasch and Nimzowitsch would stand on its own as a classic purely for its aesthetic beauty, but the enmity makes it even more significant. On move 28, with Nimzowitsch's position hopeless, Tarrasch had a straightforward way to checkmate in three moves.

But instead, he decided to toy with his vanquished opponent for a while, like a cat playing with a mouse before putting it out of its misery. *Schadenfreude* is a German word which means "pleasure derived from someone else's pain", and Tarrasch wasn't about to pass up the opportunity to experience some. He relished twisting the knife into Nimzowitsch for that bit longer as he delivered a striking mate in five.

Marshall Defense

1.	d4	d5
2.	c4	Nf6

Frank Marshall was a United States chess master of the early 20th century, a time when the young American nation was growing up. Railroads were crisscrossing the continent to deliver its bountiful natural resources to teeming factories and ports, wondrous inventions were being discovered, and in 1895 the USA became the world's leading country for manufacturing output.

The shift of geopolitical power from Europe to America came at a similar time as the United States was growing in importance in the chess world. The first five world chess championships were held in North America, thanks largely to Steinitz's move from Austria to the United States. 1886 saw Steinitz face Zukertort in three US cites; 1889 pitted Steinitz against Chigorin in Cuba; 1891 was Steinitz versus Gunsberg in New York City; 1892 was another Steinitz–Chigorin affair in Cuba; and 1894 saw Lasker finally wrest the title from Steinitz in a tour of Canadian and American cities.

Most of the best chess players were still European, but Steinitz's arrival meant the American Chess Congress were the ones who organized the first universally recognized world chess championship, and Steinitz's challengers had to cross the Atlantic to face him.

Frank Marshall's one shot at the world title occurred in 1907, the first championship match to be held in 10 years. Lasker was virtually retired from chess to concentrate on his doctoral studies in mathematics. Marshall would have fancied his chances, but he was humbled on his home turf losing eight games, drawing seven, and winning zero. In his own autobiography, Marshall barely mentions the match.

Marshall's Defense is considered unsound these days. It demonstrates the foibles of playing openings in the wrong move order. Even though playing Nf6 will probably be part of Black's plan at some point of the Queen's Gambit Declined, doing so immediately is easy to exploit. After **3. cxd5   Nxd5**, Black's knight can be chased away with tempo when White plays a pawn to e4.

Position after 3. ...Nxd5. White will claim the center by playing a pawn to e4.

In 1915, Marshall founded and gave his name to the Marshall Chess Club in New York City and led it until his death in 1944. Marshall's name appears on several other opening moves too: variously, the Marshall Variation of the French Defense, the Marshall Gambit in the Scandinavian Defense, and the Marshall Attack in the Ruy López. The name of this **2. ...Nf6** move in the Queen's Gambit Declined was given after Marshall tried it in a 1925 game against Alexander Alekhine, lost, and gave it up.

Rubinstein Variation

1.	e4	e6
2.	d4	d5
3.	Nc3	dxe4

Akiba Rubinstein, the youngest of 12 children, was in training to become a rabbi, but when he learned chess at 16 he became so smitten that he decided to abandon his studies and devote himself entirely to the game. He willed himself at his self-appointed task to become one of the world's best chess players in the early decades of the 20th century. His consistency in tournament play and head-to-head record against other leading masters made him one of the obvious challengers for the world title, but due to a combination of misfortune and bad timing, Rubinstein never got his chance.

Back then, the incumbent champion Emanuel Lasker was handpicking his challengers. Part of the bargain was that a world championship hopeful needed to raise a substantial prize purse before Lasker would accept a challenge. This was beyond a man like Rubinstein – his single-minded pursuit of chess left no time for fund-raising.

Finally, unable to ignore Rubinstein's credentials, Lasker accepted a challenge scheduled for October 1914. However, this match never took place due to the outbreak of World War I. This robbed Rubinstein of four of his best years, and he was never quite the same post-1918, eclipsed first by José Raúl Capablanca and then by Alexander Alekhine.

Unless a player wins the world chess championship, writing an influential book is a necessity to earn an opening name, with only rare exceptions. Rubinstein is one such exception, for he never left behind a literary legacy. He invented openings and was apparently satisfied enough to use these advantages to beat his opponents, rather than write about them. Understandable, for burning candles long into the night to come up with novelties in the opening is wasted effort if you reveal these discoveries to your toughest opposition.

Rubinstein left it to others to describe what he was doing in the openings, which they duly did. Today, many variations are named for him. Decades later, grandmaster Boris Gelfand even went so far as to say, "Most of the modern openings are based on Rubinstein."

This variation of the French Defense is illustrative of Rubinstein's remarkable foresight. He was an extremely talented endgame player and would select openings that led to the sorts of endgames he excelled most at. This thinking – to begin a game of chess with the end already in mind – was far ahead of its time.

In his later years, Rubinstein showed symptoms associated with schizophrenia and anthropophobia. He grew pathologically shy. While waiting for his opponent to make a move, he was known to go and cower in a corner. Losing a game became something he became unable to cope with. He retired from competitive chess in 1932 and spent the last 29 years of his life variously institutionalized and being cared for by family.

Despite these health problems and his early departure from chess, in 1950 the international chess federation (FIDE) named Rubinstein one of the 27 inaugural grandmasters, in honor of his former strength. A 1995 book called Rubinstein the *Uncrowned King*, as possibly the best player to have never won the world title.

Alekhine's Defense

1. e4   Nf6

No other chess opening so perfectly captures the personality of the man it is named after as Alekhine's Defense. Alexander Alekhine was the fourth world champion and was an unorthodox character, even by chess standards.

Serious players of the early 20th century would have been incredulous if they saw **1. ...Nf6**, but when Alekhine kept winning with it against top opposition, everyone realized the move could no longer be dismissed with a casual wave of the hand.

The opening seems highly implausible at first. The main line sees White make the obvious advance **2. e5**, chasing the knight with a near forced **2. ...Nd5**. Then, White can choose to keep harassing with **3. c4**, compelling the knight all the way over to the other side of the board from where it started; **3. ...Nb6**.

Though not normal, next move White even has the option of **4. c5**, which will mean the well-traveled knight must again find a new square.

Position after 4. c5. In this line, Black's knight will need to move four times in the first four moves.

Alekhine's Defense breaks two of opening theory's most important dictums: "do not move your pieces more than once in the opening" and "control the center". Black has moved the same knight two, three or even four times and given up complete control of the center to White by allowing all these pawn moves with tempo.

The Alekhine Defense is not just played in the hope of springing a trick on the unwary. Although White is ceded a clear space advantage, White's advanced center pawns form a broad target for Black to attack.

Even after decades of analysis, it remains unclear which player this favors. Deep study of the Alekhine Defense is like teasing out the thoughts of a mad genius.

Alekhine had been born into an aristocratic Russian family, a fact which placed him in the firing line when the Communist revolution of 1917 took hold. He fled to France and competed under the French flag in the latter half of his career. Eventually he was granted full French citizenship.

To say Alekhine was "obsessed" by chess wouldn't be doing him justice. He spent every waking moment on it, and lost all interest in social contact. When he wasn't playing, he was studying. When he wasn't studying, he was writing. Once invited to a theater performance, he sat completely disinterested in the production unfolding on the stage, preferring to play (against himself) with his pocket chess set. He even named his cats "Chess" and "Checkmate"!

Alekhine won his world title in 1927 from José Raúl Capablanca of Cuba. Apart from chess, the two men really had nothing in common. Picture the opposite of Alekhine – charming, naturally relaxed, sartorially splendid and dashingly handsome – that was Capablanca.

Alekhine's victory against the Cuban came as a surprise to most, not least to the players themselves. Capablanca was so confident that he barely even bothered preparing, and even Alekhine regarded himself as unlikely to win. Alekhine had never beaten Capablanca before the 1927 title contest, and the defending world champion had recently enjoyed an amazing eight year undefeated streak between 1916 and 1924. Yet Alekhine's single-minded work ethic saw his challenge succeed. Having beaten his rival once, Alekhine was accused of dodging Capablanca's desire for a rematch and often went out of his way to avoid tournaments Capablanca was playing in.

Alekhine's reign as world champion was punctuated by a shock loss to Max Euwe in 1935. Alekhine was struggling with alcoholism and matters were not helped by the fact the match was held in the Netherlands (Euwe's home country) where the Dutch hosts slyly plied Alekhine with as much free champagne as he wanted. After losing his crown, Alekhine sobered up, refocused, and crushed the Dutchman in the 1937 rematch.

The darkest stain on Alekhine's character comes from his links to the Nazis during World War II. He played in seven tournaments in Germany while the conflict was raging. But worst of all, a series of articles titled

Aryan Chess and Jewish Chess was written under Alekhine's name, denouncing the way Jews played chess as empty, cowardly, and materialistic, thus supporting exactly the kind of propaganda the Nazis were spreading about the Jewish people in general.

These writings blasted Steinitz and Lasker (both Jews) for playing too defensively, which unfortunately had a kernel of truth to it – their positional play <u>was</u> in fact more defensive than the attacking style of the romantic era that had preceded them. It also blamed the hypermodern movement (and the many Jewish adherents, including Nimzowitsch and Réti) for nearly destroying the game with what was termed "cheap bluff" and a "fear to struggle".

As soon as Europe was liberated from the Nazis, Alekhine publicly disavowed the articles and even denied ever writing them, contending he had been forced to publish them in his name by the occupying forces. Evidence to the contrary emerged when the original copies of the articles were later found in Alekhine's own handwriting. It remains contentious whether this anti-Semitism was what Alekhine truly believed, or if these words were penned under duress.

In March 1946, a world championship match was organized between Alekhine and a challenger from the USSR, Mikhail Botvinnik. But before the match could take place, Alekhine took the world championship title to the grave by dropping dead in his hotel room, aged 53. Some say it was a heart attack, some say he choked on his dinner, but the more sinister version of the story tells of a murder most foul carried out by the Soviet KGB to secure the world title for their own man.

Grünfeld Defense

1.	d4	Nf6
2.	c4	g6
3.	Nc3	d5

Ernst Grünfeld of Austria was born into poverty. He lost a leg early in his life, a disability which rather restricted his choice of activities. An account from Hans Kmoch describes his tragedy: "While other children played, he could only watch; while other young men found romance, he could only sit silently by... He remained handicapped in education, conversation, behaviour, and the ability to earn a livelihood."

Fortunately, Grünfeld found chess. He studied it ardently and became a respected player at his local club. Austere circumstances in post-World War I Austria made travel difficult, but he kept practicing through correspondence games through the mail.

Though his modest means did not permit him the luxury of a proper library, he collected notes on whatever available scraps of paper he could find. Grünfeld's hard work and excellent memory soon earned him a reputation as an authority on chess openings. He lived for decades in a tiny Vienna flat with his wife and daughter, and filled one room entirely with his books and writings about chess, including some 40 filing cabinets.

The Grünfeld Defense is a key hypermodern opening which became famous when Grünfeld beat a Serbian master named Boris Kostić in 1922 at Teplitz-Schönau (in the modern-day Czech Republic). Grünfeld also used the same opening later that year to defeat the future world champion, Alexander Alekhine. It is frequently said that Alekhine ended this game in spectacular fashion; rather than dipping his king in resignation, he picked the piece up and hurled it across the room! Now that's how to go out in style.

Though Grünfeld competed regularly on the international circuit in the 1920s, wins over men of Alekhine's caliber were rare. Grünfeld mainly played solid openings which seldom troubled his sternest opponents. One of his weaknesses was he invariably played **1. d4** as White because he considered any other first move to be a "mistake". This lack of variety made it significantly easier for others to prepare for games against him.

Grünfeld was more than a little eccentric. Once, he woke at four o'clock and was aghast, for he knew he had a game to play at five o'clock that day. He rushed outside, and when a tram didn't come immediately, took it upon himself to walk the whole way to the tournament venue (not easy, remember, for he had just one leg). Only once he arrived did he realize his mistake: the tournament was to start at five o'clock in the evening, but Grünfeld had turned up at five o'clock in the morning.

Réti Opening

1. Nf3   d5
2. c4

Richard Réti is remembered as one of the foremost hypermodern chess players. After World War I, Réti and others challenged the established creed of Wilhelm Steinitz and Siegbert Tarrasch that the center necessarily needed to be occupied to be controlled. They instead had the idea that control could be exerted in the opening through pawns and pieces on the flank.

David Shenk's book *The Immortal Game* makes the fascinating case that chess and society at large seem to have mirrored each other's development. Nowhere is this more apparent than the way the hypermodern movement in chess developed in the 1920s; it was a period when modernism became popular in the art world, when new forms of entertainment were exploding through film and literature, and when radical political viewpoints were taking root. Everywhere, the old order was crumbling, and fresh ideas stood ready to replace them – including in chess.

Réti laid down his beliefs in his seminal work, *Modern Ideas in Chess*. This book traced the evolution of the game from the time of Paul Morphy to the beginning of hypermodernism, and is still considered required reading for aspiring chess masters.

The Réti Opening is certainly one in the spirit of hypermodernism. If Black captures with **2. ...dxc4**, White will claim the center with **3. e4**. It was named when Réti dealt José Raúl Capablanca his first loss in eight years at the 1924 New York tournament. The move order in that game is not exactly the Réti Opening shown here, but back then almost any game that White began with Nf3 and c4 was called a "Réti".

Position after 3. e4.

Réti's career started less successfully than his later achievements. His worst tournament was Vienna, 1908 where he managed a rather inglorious 16 losses, three draws and no wins from his 19 games, finishing last, a full 4 ½ points behind the second-worst performer. That he could recover from such a dire result and become one of the world's foremost chess masters should serve as an inspiration to us all. Unfortunately, Réti's star shone all too briefly: he died aged just 40 of scarlet fever. Aside from his opening, he is also survived by several famous chess puzzles.

Nimzowitsch Defense

1. e4　　Nc6

Aron Nimzowitsch was born in Riga (in present-day Latvia) in 1886 and was introduced to chess by his father, who was one of the best players in the city. The elder Nimzowitsch had made a fortune in the timber trade and wanted Aron to join the family business, but the young man cared little for the life of a merchant and only wanted to spend his time playing chess.

When it became clear that Aron wouldn't be following in his father's footsteps, he instead went away to a German university to study mathematics and philosophy. But Aron's studies bored him and he spent most of his time in chess cafés.

Nimzowitsch entered his first international tournaments, did well, and had a promising chess career to look forward to. But around this time, World War I hit. Riga was devastated and Nimzowitsch's family lost much of their fortune. So, like many chess masters, Nimzowitsch headed to Scandinavia, which had been untouched by the conflict. There, he made a good living from giving private chess lessons, delivering lectures, and playing in simultaneous matches.

Nimzowitsch is best known as the foremost hypermodern player. Some argue the genesis of the entire hypermodern school of chess can be traced back to a single 1904 game Nimzowitsch played against Siegbert Tarrasch. Tarrasch was more than 20 years Nimzowitsch's senior and was a highly-respected figure in chess. Early in the game, Tarrasch leaned back, looked at the result of Nimzowitsch's rather unconventional opening play and exclaimed: "Never in my life have I had such a won game after 10 moves as I have now!" Nimzowitsch never forgot the insult. From then on, the two men engaged in bitter argument, mostly played out in publicly-read columns, about what constituted "proper" chess: Tarrasch's old-school "positional" style, or Nimzowitsch's radical new "hypermodern" movement.

When Nimzowitsch's career started, opening theory

was based on symmetrical center pawn formations, so playing a knight out on the first move was quite groundbreaking. In the space of just a couple of decades, Nimzowitsch and others like Richard Réti and Savielly Tartakower had proven that moves like these in the opening were perfectly playable.

These days, the Nimzowitsch Defense proper is unusual. Far more common is the "Nimzo-Indian", a variation of the Indian Defense that Nimzowitsch pioneered as a response for Black to **1. d4**, with a similar flank philosophy.

1.	d4	Nf6
2.	c4	e6
3.	Nc3	Bb4

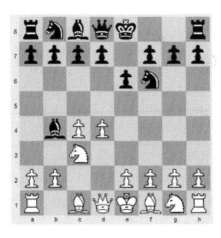

The Nimzo-Indian Defense after three moves.

Nimzowitsch was extremely patient in the

middlegame and was particularly adept at giving his opponent difficult choices. If a game can be steered towards a situation where you have many possible decent moves but your opponent must keep finding a single correct move, then they will probably make a mistake eventually. One of Nimzowitsch's favorite strategies was to overprotect his position, and to wait for his opponent to do something rash out of frustration.

His personality was rather over-sensitive and irritable. Once, when Nimzowitsch lost a game at a blitz tournament, he stood up on the table and yelled "Why must I lose to this idiot?!" Many of us have felt such an urge after a particularly galling loss, but it takes a special type of gumption to follow through and actually commit the act!

In 1929, Nimzowitsch placed first at a very strong tournament in Carlsbad (in the modern-day Czech Republic). His playing strength made him a clear candidate to challenge for the world championship, but he couldn't raise the necessary stake to secure a match with Alexander Alekhine, especially with the world in the grips of the Great Depression.

Nimzowitsch declined in playing strength after that and died of pneumonia a few years later, aged 48. He was never world champion, but through his writings and advocacy for revolutionary openings, his influence on chess has still been extremely profound.

Najdorf Variation

1.	e4	c5
2.	Nf3	d6
3.	d4	cxd4
4.	Nxd4	Nf6
5.	Nc3	a6

Miguel Najdorf of Poland was tutored in chess by his countryman, Savielly Tartakower, who Najdorf always referred to as "my teacher". Growing to be one of Poland's leading players, Najdorf represented his country at chess olympiads, part of a team of four representing his national flag.

Najdorf's life was turned upside down at the 1939 chess olympiad in Argentina. Europe in 1939 was a tinderbox, ready to explode. German provocation was met with military threats from the British and French. Britain had entered a defense pact with Poland which some thought might prevent any further German expansionism, but on 1 September 1939, news filtered through to the chess players in Buenos Aires that German soldiers had broken through the Polish border and a full-scale invasion was underway.

The English team decided to return home at once, but the other teams stayed. The confused players and administrators now had a decision to make. Given events, could the chess tournament continue? Several of the most important matches still to be played were between nations who were now on opposite sides of the war. After a lot of stressful deliberation, the decision was made to play on, albeit with the most politically charged matches not being played (such as Germany vs. Poland and Germany vs. France) and instead scored as 2–2 ties.

Germany finished in first place, half a point ahead of Najdorf's Poland. Najdorf won a gold medal for his individual performance, but chess was now of scant importance compared with events in Europe. The Soviet Union had begun an invasion of Poland of its own from the east. The Polish were hopelessly unable to fight a war on two fronts against both the German *Wehrmacht* and the Soviet Red Army and quickly capitulated. Najdorf's homeland was now partitioned roughly in half between German and Soviet spheres of influence previously agreed in secret under the

Molotov-Ribbentrop Pact.

Najdorf was Jewish, and was well aware of the reputation of the Nazis. So instead of returning to Poland after the tournament was over, he stayed in Argentina. With nothing more than the contents of his luggage, which had been packed in expectation of being away for just a few short weeks, Najdorf had to forge a new life. He played in several strong South American tournaments while the war raged, having many fellow European-in-exile chess masters for company.

Tragically, Najdorf proved to be all too correct about the dangers he would have faced as a Jew in occupied Poland. His wife, daughter, parents, and four brothers were all killed in the Holocaust. Once hostilities had finally ceased, the international chess federation was eager to resume competition and Najdorf was still a very strong player. By now an Argentine citizen, he represented his new home another 11 times.

Najdorf pioneered this variation of the Sicilian Defense through his play in the 1940s, 1950s and 1960s. The little move **5... a6** may look insignificant, but it is the start of one of the deepest wells in all chess opening theory. It prevents White's knights from landing on b5, and prepares Black for possible pawn breaks on b5 and e5. Playing the Najdorf

Variation is an examination of ability to be precise in the many complicated continuations that branch from it.

Defying the calamities his earlier life had dealt him, Najdorf won many admirers for his lively personality and linguistic élan, having picked up a healthy dose from his mentor Tartakower. He remained competitive in chess well into his old age.

Pirc Defense

1. e4   d6
2. d4   Nf6
3. Nc3

"Vasja Pirc" is a name that everybody gets wrong. Normally when a foreign name is Anglicized, the English spelling is suggestive of its pronunciation. Not so for Pirc – his name is correctly articulated as "Peerts", not "Perk". Due to the reorganization of national borders over the course of the 20th century, a quick history lesson is necessary to explain where Pirc came from.

Pirc was born in the Austro-Hungarian Empire, which was a union between the kingdoms of Austria and Hungary and the lands they had annexed. When the empire found itself on the losing side of World War I, it dissolved.

Yugoslavia was formed when some of the old

empire's lands were joined by some new areas. Pirc won the national chess championship of Yugoslavia five times and died a Yugoslav in 1980. But just over a decade later, Yugoslavia itself fragmented into several independent countries because of inter-ethnic tensions and the collapse of the former heavy-handed regime. Now the area in which Pirc spent his life is known as Slovenia.

Pirc's best chess was in the 1930s. He was the sort of player who was good enough to be invited to the top tournaments, but not so strong that he would win them. Still, he played plenty of chess against the game's leading lights including Max Euwe, Savielly Tartakower, Aron Nimzowitsch, Emanuel Lasker and Alexander Alekhine.

World War II saw Pirc's home city of Ljubljana occupied by the Axis forces. The war put a stop to European chess tournaments, so Pirc contented himself by meeting every Tuesday with another local grandmaster, Milan Vidmar. Over the course of the war they reportedly played around 1,000 games.

When international competition finally resumed, Pirc represented Yugoslavia. His country hosted and won the ninth chess olympiad in 1950 – the first olympiad held since the fateful 1939 tournament which trapped all those players in Argentina at the war's outbreak (see the chapter on Najdorf for that story).

The Pirc Defense sees White establish himself in the center, which Black aims at from the sides. The Classical line of the Pirc Defense sees Black continue with a kingside fianchetto:

3. ... g6
4. Nf3 Bg7

Position after 4. ...Bg7.

This series of moves had been seen sporadically in the 1800s, but was considered irregular. Calling an opening "irregular" is the deepest insult that can be levelled at it, usually reserved for moves like **1. b4** and **1. g4**. But Vasja Pirc was convinced that this opening had merit and could give Black a fine game. Largely through his writing and results, he succeeded in gaining a following for it, leading to the chess world to bestow Pirc's name on it.

By the 1960s, the Pirc Defense had well and truly been reclassified as playable. Pirc's heart must have swelled with pride when he lived to see his opening played in game 17 of the 1972 world chess championship between Bobby Fischer and Boris Spassky, who played as White and Black respectively. Incidentally, the game finished drawn.

But everyone still messes up Pirc's surname. Even though you now know better, I bet you have still been pronouncing it "perk" in your head the whole time you have been reading this.

Torre Attack

1.	d4	Nf6
2.	Nf3	e6
3.	Bg5	

The Torre Attack is an uncomplicated opening offering White easy development. The man it is named after, Carlos Torre Repetto, was a Mexican grandmaster. His home country is unusual in itself, because almost all the players who have had openings named after them are European. Now, as the game has globalized, we have a far more diverse set of nationalities at the top level. A look at the world's top 50 players as of the time of writing reveals players of Armenian, Chinese, Indian, Uzbekistani, and Vietnamese origin.

Sometimes a single game is all it takes for a name to be given to an opening. So it was with the Torre Attack. The highlight of his career was a 1925 win over Emanuel Lasker. Lasker had been dethroned as world champion by José Raúl Capablanca in 1921, but was still a force to be reckoned with. Nonetheless, this little-known 20-year-old from Mexico scored a famous win, which started with the first three moves that are now honored with his name.

It is probably getting a little repetitive to hear of all these chess players suffering from mental issues, but Torre was another. One contributing factor to Torre's problems may have been the actions of the woman he was due to marry; she wrote Torre a letter saying she was leaving for another man, and that was that. Torre became hospitalized in 1926 and was never quite the same.

At least, unlike others, Torre's psychological problems didn't send him to an early grave. He was even declared a grandmaster in 1977, over 50 years after the peak of his playing strength.

Grob's Attack

1. g4

Henri Grob came from Switzerland, a nation with a reputation for safe banking and reliable watchmaking. However, the ostentatious opening **1. g4** could not be more out of character with the Swiss stereotype. It thrusts forward a flank pawn with a devil-may-care attitude. Grob's Attack therefore better reflects the man than his homeland – he was a portrait painter and was married nine times over his lifetime (!).

One of the standard replies by Black is **1. ...d5**, immediately threatening White's advanced pawn with Black's light-squared bishop. White may choose to ignore the threat and fianchetto their own bishop with **2. Bg2**, x-raying an attack on Black's b7 pawn and threatening to trap Black's a8 rook. This dynamic can lead to a sharp game early with, for instance, **2.**

...Bxg4, 3. c4.

Position after 3. c4.

Grob played in several high level international tournaments from the 1920s to the 1950s where he would usually hold his own without dominating. But it is in correspondence chess that Grob really left his mark: he played over 3,000 games against readers of the Swiss newspaper *Neue Zürcher Zeitung,* often starting with his eponymous opening. He even wrote a book dedicated to **1. g4,** *Grob's Angriff* (English: "Grob's Attack").

Correspondence chess has faded in popularity since Henri Grob's time, partly because the availability of unbeatable chess computers makes it impossible to know whether the other side is playing fair. It is all too easy to have a machine churning through billions of possible moves when a correspondence chess player has days to make their move and the opponent isn't in the room.

The machines are not going to be fooled by a move like **1. g4**, but human opponents very well could be. For the adventurous chess player, there are few pleasures in life like winning with a so-called "irregular" opening like Grob's Attack.

Larsen's Opening

1. b3

Jørgen Bent Larsen was an imaginative Danish grandmaster with a penchant for offbeat openings. Samuel Reshevsky said of him: "He is a firm believer in the value of surprise. Consequently, he often resorts to dubious variations of various openings. He also likes to complicate positions even though it may involve considerable risk. He has a great deal of confidence in his game and fears no-one."

The opening that bears Larsen's name is a prime example of his unorthodox style. Larsen was inspired to try **1. b3** by the play of Aron Nimzowitsch, who, however, preferred the b-pawn push on move two after first playing **1. Nf3**. Larsen used the immediate **1. b3** often enough to get his name associated with it, thanks to his high profile and the move's relative unpopularity with anyone else.

Besides "Larsen's Opening", **1. b3** has been called the purely descriptive "Queen's Fianchetto Opening" and the playful "Baby Orangutan" – the latter moniker due to **1. b4** being known as the "Orangutan Opening" (see the later chapter in the book for why) and **1. b3** representing a lesser pawn advance than the Orangutan proper.

A fianchettoed queen's bishop can be an asset for White, but it grants Black a lot of freedom to be proactive in the center. This was, in fact, part of Larsen's unusual philosophy: if Black expects to rely on their well-memorized opening responses, he can find himself at a loss when granted the initiative unexpectedly. Modern players remain skeptical of Larsen's Opening, but the move has a certain shock value and isn't completely devoid of threats.

Larsen was frequently mentioned alongside Bobby Fischer as the only players from the West that the elite Soviet players feared during the height of their 20th century chess dominance. In the 1970 USSR vs. Rest of the World match, Larsen played for the Rest of the World on board 1 (ahead of Fischer) and achieved a positive 2 ½ points out of 4. During the 1970 interzonal tournament, Larsen was the only man to beat Bobby Fischer in 23 games, but Fischer crushed Larsen in the semifinals of the subsequent 1971 candidates tournament by 6–0.

Benko Gambit

1.	d4	Nf6
2.	c4	c5
3.	d5	b5

Pal Benko was born in France, raised in Hungary, and moved to the United States in 1957. There, he made his name as a chess master, puzzle composer and author. He was the winner or joint winner of the US Open chess championship eight times. While he never won through to play for the world championship, Benko did play an important role in helping one of his compatriots get there.

To qualify to face the reigning world champion requires winning a candidates tournament made up of other aspiring challengers. From the 1950s to 1990s, qualification for the candidates tournament was determined through an interzonal tournament. In turn, to qualify for the interzonal tournament, a player had to perform well in the championship of their own home country.

By the late 1960s, it was clear that the young Bobby Fischer was America's best hope of capturing the world crown. The US chess authorities tried to get Fischer to play at the 1969 US championship and thus set him on the path to a potential shot at the title, but Fischer refused the invitation because he felt the tournament was too short.

In Fischer's own words: "I want very much to play in the US championship this year – but not in a tournament where if a player has a bad start and loses a game or two at the beginning, he is practically eliminated from first place. I consider this to be too chancy an affair and it puts an undue burden on the favorite, who does not have enough time to make up for a bad start because the tournament is so short. Our US championship is the shortest of any major chess country. It is an affront to any professional chess player – such as I am."

The organizers urged the tempestuous Fischer to reconsider, but he was not one to back down once he had made up his mind. The tournament came and went without Fischer, and the highest three finishers qualified for the interzonal tournament: Sammy Reshevsky, William Addison and Pal Benko.

Benko had already been to two candidates tournaments, finishing eighth in 1959 and sixth in 1962. He decided to give up his spot in the interzonal to someone who had a better chance of going all the way – Fischer. Sure enough, Bobby Fischer went on to sweep all before him in the 1970 interzonal tournament, in the 1971 candidates tournament, and in the 1972 world championship contest against Boris Spassky.

As for the Benko Gambit, **3. ...b5** offers up a pawn with the promise of breaking up White's pawn center. In Eastern Europe, it had long been known as the "Volga Gambit" after a 1946 article about it was published in the Soviet Union city of Kuybyshev (now Samara) which sits on the Volga River.

Benko used the move in top level play and promoted it through a book he published in 1974, self-titling it The Benko Gambit. Given the cultural sway America held over the rest of the Western world, the name "Benko Gambit" came to supplant the old Volga Gambit name in English-speaking countries.

Fischer Defense

1. e4	e5
2. f4	exf4
3. Nf3	d6

Bobby Fischer was a phenomenon – temperamental, reclusive, and brilliant. Despite winning just a single world championship, he is frequently cited as one of the greatest chess players of all time. Certainly, no world championship match before or since has generated anything close to the level of public interest as the 1972 event between Fischer and Boris Spassky.

Fischer famously derided the King's Gambit as unsound for White. He believed Black need only accept the offered pawn on f4 and play **3. ...d6** to be better. This move became known as the Fischer Defense and these days the King's Gambit is rare in games between top grandmasters, due in large part to Fischer.

Growing up in Brooklyn, New York City, Fischer was hooked on chess from a young age. He became completely devoted to its study and even learned Russian just so he could read the latest developments in their chess magazines. At 14 he won his first of eight US championships. Aged 15 years, six months and one day he became the youngest grandmaster ever. He dropped out of high school at 16, the earliest legal opportunity to do so, later saying: "You don't learn anything at school."

Controversy was never far from Fischer. He would frequently accuse the USSR players of colluding (which, it is generally agreed, they were). He would demand changes to the playing conditions, he would demand more money, and he would refuse to play if these demands weren't met.

Entire books, films, and even a West End musical have been produced about what happened in the 1972 world chess championship. Both players were under an unusual pressure to win, not just for themselves, and not just for their countries, but for the capitalist and communist ideologies. Just three years earlier, the United States had won the space race when Neil Armstrong took his one small step upon the surface of the Moon. Now, this lone wolf American challenger was ready to take on the Soviet chess machine, long held as a powerful exemplar of socialist discipline and mental superiority over the decadent West. Fischer's American individualism versus Spassky's state-sponsored might and power. It was billed as "The Match of the Century", and deservedly so. Fischer himself was keen to embrace the symbolism, remarking "This little thing between me and Spassky is bigger than Frazier and Ali. It's the free world against the lying, cheating hypocritical Russians."

Fischer lost the first game by falling for an elementary trap more regularly seen by rank beginners: the "poisoned pawn", where a bishop captures an apparently undefended enemy pawn, but then finds itself unable to escape. Perhaps shaken by his blunder, Fischer demanded that the television cameras be removed from the playing hall before he would play again. When the tournament organizers refused, Fischer didn't show up to play the second game and thus fell behind by another point, by forfeit.

Down 2–0, Fischer was all set to quit the tournament. Allegedly, it took a call from the United States National Security Advisor Henry Kissinger to convince him to stay, such was the geopolitical importance the match had assumed.

For his part, Spassky must have been feeling more

than a little bemused by Fischer's irascible behavior. Rather than win by default, Spassky acceded to Fischer's demands for the removal of the cameras. Fischer then proceeded to win five of the next eight games, several in stunning fashion, and eventually triumphed decisively by a final margin of 12 ½ to 8 ½.

Fischer was fêted as a hero upon his return to the United States. He appeared on the cover of *Sports Illustrated*. He received offers for product endorsements worth millions of dollars, all of which he refused. Chess underwent an incredible surge in popularity thanks to Fischer-mania.

But when it came time to organize his 1975 title defense, things began to unravel. Fischer again made many demands on the organizers. Several of these were granted, but Fischer was adamant that he would not play unless all his conditions were met. In the end, the international chess federation gave up on trying to compromise with the petulant American, and awarded the championship by default to the challenger, Anatoly Karpov. The world title was back in Soviet hands, where it remained for the rest of the Cold War.

Fischer faded from the spotlight and chess moved on without him. Then in 1992 he suddenly re-emerged in Yugoslavia to play a bizarre series of games against

Boris Spassky, his opponent from 20 years earlier. According to Fischer, these games were for the "world championship" – Fischer's reasoning was he had never been defeated, and thus was still the true world champion.

These games attracted the ire of the United States government as they were in contravention of a United Nations Security Council resolution prohibiting economic activities in Yugoslavia. Fischer was warned not to proceed, but in response, he held a press conference and literally spat on the US order. A warrant was issued for Fischer's arrest. He made his way to the site of his 1972 triumph, Iceland, which granted him citizenship and asylum.

Fischer grew to hate America. He applauded the 9/11 terrorist attacks on his home city of New York. He was also known for his extraordinary anti-Semitic tirades, a fact made all the stranger by the fact his mother was born to Jewish parents, meaning Bobby Fischer himself had Jewish blood.

The parallels between Fischer and his 19th century compatriot, Paul Morphy, are impossible to ignore. Both men were prodigious junior talents. Both dominated all competition in the United States. Both then set out to conquer the established order: for Morphy, the European masters; for Fischer: the Soviet

Union's stranglehold on the world title. Both stormed to famous wins that captured the American public's imagination. And then, having climbed the Everest of the chess world, both men promptly disappeared from the public eye and suffered a life of misfortune thereafter.

The Places

Most historians believe chess began in India, spread to Persia, and then continued to Europe, settling on something resembling today's rules around the year 1500. Other variants of the game have continued elsewhere, including *Chaturanga* (Indian chess), *Xiangqi* (Chinese chess), *Makruk* (Thai chess), *Shogi* (Japanese chess), and others. Thanks to their shared ancestry, all have elements in common.

For the chess we know, Europe was the undisputed center of the world when opening names were being determined. Because of this, all but one of the opening names in this section are European cities, countries and regions.

The ordering of this section is thus: first are openings named after countries, then regions, and finally cities. I suspect that for many readers, this will offer the bonus of a geography lesson.

Next time you travel, I encourage you to try and strike up a game of chess and play the corresponding opening. Any real chess enthusiast would find a certain satisfaction from playing a Scotch Opening in Scotland, a French Defense in France, or a Budapest Gambit in Budapest.

English Opening

1. c4

The English Opening is just ever so slightly off-beat, much like the English themselves. They foment a national image of stoicism, gentle self-deprecation and keeping a stiff upper lip, yet beneath the surface are a people with a most idiosyncratic sense of humor.

1. c4 was pioneered by everybody's favorite mutton-chopped 19th century chess-playing Englishman, Howard Staunton. Staunton used the move six times when playing as White in his 1843 match against the Frenchman Saint-Amant at the Café de la Régence, although with mixed results. Staunton won the first two times he tried it, but Saint-Amant got better with experience and Staunton could only draw two and lose two of the next four games where he started with **1. c4**.

Today, the English Opening is White's fourth most popular choice of the 20 possible first moves, but for many years it was given no respect at all. Ruy López noticed **1. c4** centuries ago and thought it so bad that no player of any skill would use it. Staunton's peers in the 1800s thought it was a bit strange too, and it didn't catch on with others, despite Staunton's influence.

The hypermodern school of chess meant that interest in **1. c4** grew in the early 20th century. If flank attacks like the Sicilian Defense could work for Black, then why not for White? Another advantage of the English Opening lies in its flexibility – it has strong potential to transpose to other openings, depending on what Black does.

A chess game can last hours, and keeping one's concentration throughout this mental marathon has always been a key test of a player's mettle. However, some of Staunton's 19th century compatriots took things to an extreme. In the days before chess clocks, each player could take as long as he liked to ponder their move before making it, leading to games of ten hours, twenty hours, or even more.

The Even More Complete Chess Addict recounts the encounters between Elijah Williams and James Mucklow at the 1851 London tournament where both players were on the verge of falling asleep, such was the lengthiness of their contemplation. It got so bad that one of the games needed to be adjourned for an evening so that everyone could go to bed. Howard Staunton wrote of the two men, "Each... exhibits the same want of depth and inventive power in his combinations, and the same tiresome prolixity in maneuvering his men. It need hardly be said that the games, from first to last, are remarkable only for their unvarying and unexampled dullness."

Scotch Opening

1. e4 e5
2. Nf3 Nc6
3. d4

Like the drink that bears its name, the Scotch is a rich, flavorsome way to play. It is an uncomplicated and direct opening, much like the stereotypical Scotsman.

The separate kingdoms of Scotland and England joined to form the United Kingdom in 1707. England has always been the dominant force within the union with the much larger population of the two. Still, the Scots maintain a distinct character of their own and there is nothing they love more than beating the English.

In 1824, Edinburgh, the capital of Scotland, challenged London to a chess match. London was a little taken aback by the temerity of Edinburgh, for the upstart Scottish club had only been formed a couple of years prior. Yet here they were, throwing down the gauntlet to the most eminent players of Britain's largest city. Nevertheless, the challenge was accepted. The match took place by mail correspondence, a terribly slow business in those days, before inter-city rail transport and the invention of the telegraph. Each move needed to travel the hundreds of miles back and forth between London and Edinburgh by horse and carriage.

The clubs played five games between 1824 and 1828. The games were published in newspapers and keenly observed by the public like sports are today. Everybody expected a lopsided victory for London, but the Scots surprisingly prevailed. Three of the five games started with what we now call the Scotch Opening, including the decisive fifth game where Edinburgh played it as White and won. Their victory was sealed, two wins to one, and the opening came to be known as the Scotch.

During the second game, London controversially tried to retract a move after it had been mailed. The post office refused London's attempts to stop the letter's delivery. Then, Edinburgh refused to acquiesce when they received the original move and London's second letter pleading for an alteration. Edinburgh went on to win the game.

The Scotch Opening allows for easy piece development. The d4 pawn is pushed ahead boldly, and normally provokes **3. ...exd4** from Black. The center is cleared and both sides are left with a great degree of freedom. As anyone familiar with the blockbuster film *Braveheart* will know, "freedom" was the clarion call of William Wallace in the 13th century Scottish war of independence against England. Fitting, then, that it was another battle – of the chess kind – between the two that gave the Scotch Opening its name.

French Defense

1. e4　　e6

France occupies a central place in chess history, and the French Defense is one of chess's most solid and resilient center pawn openings.

The French embraced the game like nowhere else in the 18th and early 19th century. Chess cafés were incredibly prolific there, and French players monopolized the mantle of world preeminence for generations: Legall de Kermeur, François-André Danican Philidor, Louis-Charles Mahé de La Bourdonnais, and Pierre Charles Fournier de Saint Amant all followed one another in succession until the 1840s. Today, the international chess federation is known as "FIDE", which is a French acronym for *Fédération Internationale des Échecs.* French words turn up elsewhere in the game too, such as the *en passant* pawn capture rule and *j'adoube,* said when adjusting a piece's position on a square without violating the touch-move rule.

The French Defense may seem that Black is too timid to push the pawn all the way to meet its opposite, but the next moves reveal more aggression. White usually continues with **2. d4**, which Black may meet with **2. ...d5**.

Position after 2. ...d5.

What White does next can vary, but often Black will target White's d4 pawn by playing c5 at some point – just the kind of flank attack that the French general Napoleon Bonaparte was famous for in his early conquests through Europe.

Napoleon, the Emperor of the French from 1804 to 1814, had a deep love for chess. It is, after all, a game of war, and over the years, many battle commanders have turned to chess for inspiration. On the real battlefield, Napoleon had an uncanny knack for sensing the intentions of the enemy and controlling the course of battle, but on the chess board he was mediocre at best. Perhaps the fact a military commander's prowess does not transfer to ability at chess is unsurprising – a game with fixed rules played in silence by two equal forces on a square board is a long way removed from the chaos of actual combat.

The French Defense got its name from a correspondence match between the cities of London and Paris in 1834. Chamouillet, one of the players of the Parisian team, persuaded his team to play the (at the time) quite novel **1. ...e6**, which proved to be the Londoner's undoing. For the Paris club, winning must have been particularly sweet given that France's defeat in the Napoleonic Wars was still fresh in the memory. At last, a French victory!

Dutch Defense

1. d4 f5

The Netherlands is a small northern European country known for its tulips, windmills, bicycles, canals, and wooden shoes. Strangely, the words for the country and for the people who come from there do not match up. We have Norwegians from Norway, Australians from Australia, and Japanese from Japan, but when it comes to "the Netherlands", we call them "Dutch". To confuse matters further, the word "Holland" is often bandied around. "Holland" (when properly used) refers to just two of the 12 provinces of the Netherlands: Noord-Holland and Zuid-Holland.

The Dutch Defense was originally named for Elias Stein, who wrote a 1789 book that recommended **1. ...f5** as the best response to **1. d4**. Stein was actually born in France and published his book in French, but because he had settled in The Hague it was the

"Dutch Defense" name that the chess world picked up.

The only time that a Dutchman won the world chess title was when Max Euwe unexpectedly defeated Alexander Alekhine in 1935. The match took place in the Netherlands, and the best-remembered game (the 26th of the match, commonly referred to as "The Pearl of Zandvoort", after the town the game took place in) was appropriately a Dutch Defense, won by Euwe, the Dutchman.

The true linkage the Dutch Defense has with the real-life Dutch lies in their shared quirkiness. These people eat chocolate sprinkles for lunch, delight in wearing blackface around Christmas time, and hold a reputation for being highly conservative with money despite their seemingly contradictory relaxed attitude to sexuality and drug use.

The Dutch Defense is similarly esoteric. Throwing the f-pawn forward on move one is not for the faint of heart. Usually Black will castle kingside, which leaves the king with no pawn on f7, representing a significant hole in Black's defensive dyke. The diagonal between c4 and g8 is often a weakness. But the Dutch have always been a nation of traders, and the compensation for Black is the opportunity to launch an immediate kingside assault. It is an exciting opening, and can throw the White **1. d4** player off balance if he were expecting a symmetrical center pawn game.

Danish Gambit

1.	e4	e5
2.	d4	exd4
3.	c3	

The Danish Gambit is named for the nation of Denmark, not the delicious sweet Danish pastries. Although, given White is inviting Black to gobble up a couple of pawns, perhaps a double entendre is at play.

The opening is most strongly associated with a Danish chess master, Martin Severin From. From was active as a player in the mid-to-late 19th century, but is better remembered as an analyst and administrator. From wrote an essay on the sequence of moves now known as the "Danish Gambit" while playing in a very strong 1867 tournament in Paris. Perhaps he penned it as a ruse to distract attention from his own play, as he came equal last out of the thirteen entrants. In a way, this makes From's achievement in immortalizing the Danish Gambit even more remarkable – it's one thing to popularize an opening thanks to winning a tournament with it, but it is surely even more challenging if the player has performed poorly.

An interesting quirk of this 1867 tournament was that it used a different scoring system to the one today's players are most familiar with. Almost universally, present-day chess tournaments award 1 point for a win, both players get ½ a point for a draw and 0 points for a loss. Chess has been scored this way for such a long time that it's hard to imagine an alternative, but other scoring systems do exist. In Paris 1867, it was 1 point for a win, <u>0 points for a draw</u> and 0 for a loss. Drawing a game was as bad as losing.

This system may hint at a solution to the scourge of modern chess; at the top level especially, there are far too many draws. When playing with the Black pieces, emerging with a draw is considered a fine result in contests between elite grandmasters, so they often try to lead the position towards a drawish end rather than play sharp lines and risk a loss. There's also the so-called "grandmaster draw" – a draw by agreement where, early in the game, both players simply agree to shake hands and share the point before things even get interesting. Such a safety-first approach is not great for the game's followers who want to see danger, excitement and decisive results.

The problem of excessive drawing is not restricted to chess. In football (soccer), goals are difficult to score, and it is tempting for teams to adopt a defensive mindset rather than press forward for a win. But spectators hate 0-0 draws, and indeed don't particularly enjoy draws of any kind. Competition is meant to be about the thrill of victory and the agony of defeat, not the melancholy of a draw.

To combat the drawing tendency, the Football League in England tried something drastic for the 1980/81 season when they increased the value of a win from 2 points to 3 points. Draws remained worth 1 point, and 0 points for a loss. A team became better off if they won one game and lost one game (3 points total) than if they drew two games (2 points).

Placing additional value on wins with respect to draws had the desired result. The number of drawn matches across the first division season fell to 25.5% of games played, compared to 29.0% in the preceding season. Observing the improvement, other national football leagues quickly followed suit and today the 3 / 1 / 0 system is ubiquitous.

Could chess embrace such a radical departure? There would be many naysayers, but 3 / 1 / 0 is already in use at the annual Bilbao Chess Masters tournament. It attracts some of the world's very strongest players and the scoring system does indeed seem to have the desired effect. By giving more points for a win, it stimulates more aggressive chess and fewer draws.

Even though the Danish Gambit is today decried as "unsound" by the experts, Martin Severin From may have been correct in recommending it, given the way the 1867 Paris tournament scoring system heavily penalized draws. Since the Danish Gambit sees White offering Black the chance to go a pawn ahead in material in exchange for White's own fast development, the position immediately becomes unbalanced and one side or the other is more likely to emerge with a win. If 3 / 1 / 0 ever becomes more widespread, we may see a revival of interest in more dangerous openings such as the Danish Gambit.

Indian Defense

1. d4   Nf6

The term "Indian Defense" was first used when referring to a game between an Indian and a Scot. The two players were Moheschunder Bannerjee and John Cochrane. From their names alone, you can probably tell which man came from where.

Cochrane was a barrister by profession. He came to be stationed in Calcutta, which in the 19th century was one of the British Empire's far-flung outposts. The trouble was, Cochrane was one of the best chess players in the entire United Kingdom. Howard Staunton regarded him as something of a father figure, and found Cochrane to be a testing adversary when they had occasion to play. But in India, far from the strongest European masters, Cochrane could find no rivals worthy of him.

That all changed in 1848 when a member of the Calcutta chess club heard tell of a local who had never been beaten. The club member asked around, tracked down this mysterious Indian and arranged a game with him. Sure enough, the club member was defeated handily. Bannerjee was more familiar with traditional Indian chess (*Chaturanga*), but also showed an uncanny aptitude for the type of chess that the British played.

Bannerjee was convinced to come back to Calcutta to play the waiting John Cochrane. Thus, it came to pass that a prominent colonial barrister and a native Bengali sat down to a game that transcended their two very different cultures. Although Cochrane won, he was mightily impressed by Bannerjee's play, and was overjoyed to finally find someone in India who could properly challenge him at the game he loved. Over the next few years, the two played hundreds of times, with Bannerjee winning enough to keep things interesting. The games were faithfully recorded by Cochrane, and the particularly notable ones were published in the London chess magazines that Cochrane wrote for.

Though the Indian Defense proper is just one move from each player, many "Indian" openings see Black *fianchetto*, where the bishop moves from its starting square to the long diagonal. For example, the "King's Indian Defense" setup sees the dark-squared Black bishop sit on g7, while the "Queen's Indian Defense" has the light-squared Black bishop move to b7.

Chaturanga is similar in many regards to the chess we play, but one of the critical differences is pawns cannot move forward two squares on their first move. This makes filling the center with pawns far more time-consuming than in regular chess. Therefore, in *Chaturanga*, placing pieces on the side of the board is a very natural way to gain control of the center without occupying it. Bannerjee applied this knowledge to the chess the British had brought with them, and regularly fianchettoed before it was fashionable to do so. He was playing flank attack setups over half a century before the hypermodern players of the early 20th century popularized them. When Cochrane's games reached Europe, Bannerjee's style came to be known as the "Indian Defense".

Chess is generally believed to have originated in India. Centuries had seen it travel from the subcontinent, through the arid Middle East, across the Mediterranean Sea, over the European continent, and finally bridged the English Channel to the cold, distant British Isles. And then, in a twist of history, these colonial British had sailed all the way back to where chess began, where they and the locals could still find shared pleasure in playing one another.

Scandinavian Defense

1. e4   d5

In the French Defense, Black plays **1. ...e6**, preparing **2. ...d5**. And in the Caro-Kann Defense, Black plays **1. ...c6**, again to support a **2. ...d5** surge. In the Scandinavian Defense, Black doesn't bother with any such groundwork and simply thrusts forward by playing **1. ...d5** immediately.

Modern Scandinavians are held up as exemplars of civilization. On the whole, they are a blond-haired, IKEA-shopping, egalitarian, politically progressive people. This belies their history, for they are descended from the bloodthirsty Vikings, who made their name by pillaging and terrorizing northern Europe during the Dark Ages. The Vikings would go forth in their fearsome longboats, set ashore, and, once they had their fill of plunder, return to their frigid homeland and drink from the skulls of their victims.

The Scandinavian Defense echoes the Scandinavian's vicious past far more than their mild-mannered present. It is a combative opening where the ill-prepared opponent can quickly be vanquished, just like the unsuspecting villagers set upon by the Vikings in days of yore. In the main line, White captures the offered pawn with **2. exd5**, Black wastes no time in recapturing with **2. ...Qxd5**, and White gains a tempo by bringing out his knight and threatening the queen: **3. Nc3.** All of this is expected by the prepared Scandinavian player. It is immediate hand-to-hand warfare.

Position after 3. Nc3.

The website chessgames.com features a vast database of recorded chess games, going back hundreds of years. The very oldest game they have on record is a Scandinavian Defense, played in Valencia, Spain in 1475. To put that in historical context, the game in question took place before Christopher Columbus had sailed to America!

The Scandinavian Defense gained its name mainly thanks to Ludvig Collijn, who served as chairman of the Swedish Chess Federation from 1917 to 1939. In his earlier days, Collijn competed at the 1897 Nordic chess championship where, as Black, he responded consistently to **1. e4** with **1. ...d5**. Collijn finished a respectable eighth in the tournament, which was incidentally won by a man called Sven Otto Svensson, which is quite possibly the most Swedish name imaginable.

But how did it come to pass that the tournament that gave the opening its name was the <u>Nordic</u> chess championship, yet <u>Scandinavian</u> was bestowed on it? It's the manifestation of an extremely common error; people often conflate "Scandinavian" and "Nordic" with each other, but in fact they are not the same. The term "Scandinavia" includes the three kingdoms of Denmark, Norway and Sweden. The languages of these countries retain enough similarities that Danes, Swedes and Norwegians all understand one another to this day. Often, outsiders mistakenly include Finns and Icelanders when referring to Scandinavians, but strictly speaking, Iceland and Finland are Nordic countries, but not Scandinavian. Finnish and Icelandic people find Scandinavian tongues incomprehensible, and as Michael Booth joked in *The Almost Nearly Perfect People*, at Nordic Council meetings, the Finns and Icelanders tend to be found in a corner away from everyone else, speaking in English to one another.

The best player Scandinavia has ever produced is the 21st century world champion Magnus Carlsen of Norway. He was a grandmaster at 13. At the same age, he managed to draw a rapid game against Garry Kasparov, the world number one at the time – a sensational result for someone so young. Carlsen continued to improve as he moved into adulthood, and he captured the coveted world crown from Vishy Anand in 2013.

In an era where computers reign supreme over elite human players, Carlsen plays the most like a machine out of anyone without a silicon brain. He thrives in the long-term strategy of the middlegame and is unbelievably tenacious in the endgame. Like a computer, he seemingly doesn't make mistakes once most of the pieces are off the board.

Carlsen doesn't play the Scandinavian Defense often –

he is very much a modern Scandinavian, with no taste for the flesh and blood of his Viking ancestors or the double-edged positions this opening is known for. He even supplements his chess earnings through fashion modelling.

Sicilian Defense

1. e4   c5

Sicily is the largest island in the Mediterranean Sea, located south of the mainland Italian Peninsula across the narrow Strait of Messina. It is one of the 20 regions of Italy, and home to Europe's tallest active volcano, Mount Etna.

In popular culture, Sicily is inextricably linked to the criminal underworld thanks to the critically acclaimed film, *The Godfather*. In it, Don Vito Corleone is the patriarch of a New York mafia family at war with four other Italian-American criminal households. One of Don Vito's sons, Michael, initially wants no part in living a life of crime, but is eventually drawn into the family's underworld activities and becomes the most ruthless Don of them all.

1. ...c5 was recommended by several Italians as a serious response to **1. e4** all the way back in the 1600s and 1700s when the only respectable move for Black was the symmetrical **1. ...e5**. Despite the long history of **1. ...c5,** the term "Sicilian Defense" was only solidified only relatively recently, in 1813. The English master Jacob Henry Sarratt referred to an old Italian manuscript calling **1. e4   c5** *Il gioco siciliano* (English: the Sicilian game), and the name stuck.

Given the mafia's reputation for violence, it is most fitting that the Sicilian Defense is one of the most murderous openings available to Black. It makes for a sharp, immediate fight as Black's c5 pawn leers at d4, and if White chooses to release the pressure it will often come at the cost of one of the two precious center pawns. The cut and thrust of the Sicilian makes it one of the most popular responses to **1. e4** by grandmasters and casual players alike. If White plays **1. e4**, then it is impossible to avoid being forced into a Sicilian Defense setup if Black desires it. As the immortal line from *The Godfather* goes, it's "an offer they can't refuse."

The theoretical development of the Sicilian runs both wide and deep: many of the other chapters in this book refer to famous sub-lines of it. The Najdorf Variation, the Dragon Variation, the Maróczy Bind –

each have had entire books written about them. If you want to play chess competently, you need to be familiar with at least the basics of the Sicilian Defense. There is no escaping it, just as Michael Corleone couldn't help but be dragged into the illicit family business in *The Godfather*.

Catalan Opening

1.	d4	Nf6
2.	c4	e6
3.	g3	

Though Catalonia is politically part of Spain, the region retains its own language and a strong identity. Over the centuries, the territory has been violently fought over and has been the scene of many tragic massacres. It has been an independent state, ruled by Spain, and ruled by France. As a result, the Catalan language includes elements of both Spanish and French.

The Catalan Opening received its name from a 1929 chess tournament held in Barcelona, the capital of Catalonia. To commemorate the event, the tournament organizers held a competition to name an original opening in its honor. The winner of this invent-an-opening contest was Savielly Tartakower, who was participating in the tournament (finishing 2nd, behind José Raúl Capablanca). Tartakower submitted the above sequence and took home the prize.

Despite its contrived invention, the Catalan Opening remains very popular today. It is a highly elastic opening where White focuses on attacking Black's queenside with the fianchettoed light-square bishop.

Just a few years later, in 1936, the Spanish Civil War erupted. Catalonia fought on the side of the Republicans against the Nationalists of General Franco, who were supported by fascist Germany and Italy. Three years of bloodshed resulted in a crushing defeat for the Republicans and harsh reprisals for those who had fought on their side. The Catalan language was banned by the new Francoist dictatorship until 1975.

These days, Barcelona is a prosperous, cosmopolitan city. Nonetheless, the issue of rule from Madrid is still a hot topic. Catalan independence protests draw hundreds of thousands of impassioned supporters waving their distinctive red and yellow flags. The prospect of breaking away to form their own country has been consistently dismissed by the Spanish central government, but calls remain.

Baltic Opening

1. Nc3

The Baltic Opening is a flexible first move. Since White will often play a knight to c3 early in the game anyway, it waits to see what Black does before committing a pawn (which cannot be taken back). It develops a knight to a central square, so it can't be considered a terrible move.

The name of the Baltic Opening is also flexible. It is also known as the Heinrichsen Opening, the Dunst Opening, van Geet's Opening, the Sleipnir Opening, Kotrč's Opening, the Meštrović Opening, the Romanian Opening, the Queen's Knight Attack, Millard's Opening, and (in German) *der Linksspringer*.

Whatever you call it, the main drawback of **1. Nc3** is that it doesn't prevent Black from occupying the center of the board however he likes. **1. Nf3** prevents **1. ...e5**, but playing **1. Nc3** does not prevent **1. ...d5** because the d5 pawn is protected by Black's queen.

The "Baltics" refer to the three countries in northern Europe on the eastern coast of the Baltic Sea: Estonia, Lithuania and Latvia. They were part of the Soviet Union until its dissolution in 1991, but today are members of NATO and the European Union. These Baltic countries had been invaded many times over the years, even before the most recent Soviet occupation, including by Sweden and by Germany. As a result, they have elements of Nordic, German and Russian culture in their food, architecture and culture.

Arved Heinrichsen, a Lithuanian from the late 19th century, is responsible for the Baltic Opening's name. He traveled from his hometown of Vilnius to Berlin to study medicine, played at a few tournaments while in Germany and became known for playing **1. Nc3**. Alas, the young man contracted tuberculosis and was sent to Egypt to recover, but picked up malaria while there. Heinrichsen died at age 20, but his memory lives on through the Baltic Opening.

Slav Defense

1.	d4	d5
2.	c4	c6

Slavs are an ethnic group native to central, eastern and southeastern Europe. Various attempts have been made to give them their own countries, usually with failed results. For example, Yugoslavia was formed to be a nation for all southern Slavic people, but exploded into ethnic conflict in the 1980s and 1990s. The Soviet Union's own Slavic lands broke apart into Russia, Ukraine and Belarus in 1991. Czechoslovakia underwent a more peaceful divorce between the Czechs and the Slovaks in 1993. Evidently, even within the "Slavic" grouping, there are important differences that prevent a common sense of identity.

The Slavic lands were crushed under the yoke of an oppressive regime after World War II. This is not the only time in their history the Slavs were oppressed:

the English word "slave" has its origins from "Slav" due to the servitude suffered at the hands of Muslim conquerors in the 9th century.

These days, their circumstances are happier and their quality of life has improved. Many Slavs maintain the tradition of playing chess in parks which has unfortunately been lost to much of the rest of the world. Their reputation as chess players is still fearsome; one of the first rules this author learned as a young man was to be leery of challenging any chess player with a Slavic-sounding name.

The Slav Defense was named because so many strong Slavic grandmasters helped to popularize it; Semyon Alapin, Alexander Alekhine, Efim Bogoljubov and Milan Vidmar all helped develop the theory behind the move. One upside of **2. ...c6** is that Black's light-squared bishop is not locked in, unlike when **2. ...e6** is played to decline the Queen's Gambit.

The central tension can be relieved right away in the Exchange Variation: **3. cxd5   cxd5**, while other lines can become very complex. The Slav Defense has survived extensive examination from the 1920s to the present day and still retains a large and respected following.

London System

1.	d4	Nf6
2.	Nf3	d5
3.	Bf4	

The London System was named after a world-class chess tournament held there in 1922. At the time, all sorts of novel openings were in vogue thanks to the new hypermodern style sweeping through chess. To counter this, the more traditional players wanted a solid way to play to get them out of the opening with minimal complications and into a playable middlegame. What they came up with came to be known as the London System. The opening shown in the above diagram is but one example – other move sequences can also be called the same, so long as they include the hallmarks: a White bishop on f4 and a White pawn on d4.

London's most important locale was Simpson's

Divan, which was a coffee house and chess club like Paris's Café de la Régence. Like its equivalent in the French capital, most of the city's 19th century luminaries passed through Simpson's Divan, including Charles Dickens, George Bernard Shaw, Sir Arthur Conan Doyle, Benjamin Disraeli and William Gladstone.

The establishment also hosted many games between the best chess players of the 1800s. Johannes Zukertort (Steinitz's opponent in the first official world chess championship) even died of a stroke suffered there! You can still visit "Simpson's-in-the-Strand" today and view an excellent museum of chess memorabilia.

London and Paris were both principal European chess centers for most of the 19th century. Paris held the ascendancy in the early 1800s. The balance only swung to the other side of the English Channel in 1851, when Howard Staunton conceived and organized the first international chess tournament of Europe's leading masters.

Aside from the games, Staunton's other main objective for the 1851 London chess tournament was to convene a chess parliament among the players present, with the aim of standardizing the rules of chess once and for all. There were still a few small regional differences which needed ironing out, the notation used to record games wasn't the same everywhere, and something had to be done about the appallingly long time that some players were taking to make their moves. These efforts resulted in the first internationally agreed code of chess laws being published in 1860.

London was the scene of another important chess innovation in 1922, shortly after José Raúl Capablanca dethroned Emanuel Lasker after a 27 year reign. Lasker's era as world champion had been extended, at least in part, by the complete freedom he enjoyed to dictate the terms under which he would meet contenders. He could set the stakes, decide the number of games to be played and even suggest the margin of required victory... in 1911 Lasker had proposed to Capablanca that the challenger needed to beat him by two games to win the title!

To avoid such controversy in the future, the 1922 London tournament saw Capablanca get together with the other leading masters to draw up a set of rules for future world championship matches. One of the most notable rules was the requirement for the match winner to achieve six wins, with drawn games not to count. This document came to be known as the "London Rules".

In 1927 Capablanca met Alekhine under these rules, and after 34 games Alekhine had the necessary six wins. That may seem like a lot of games, but an even longer contest occurred when Garry Kasparov and Anatoly Karpov met under the first-to-six-win system in 1984–85.

After nine games, the incumbent champion Karpov had raced out to a four win to zero lead and looked on course to easily defend his title. But Kasparov dug in and an extraordinary 17 successive draws followed. Finally, Karpov broke the monotony with another win to make it 5–0, but then another 14 draws followed. 32 games had taken place with only one decisive result. It was hard enough to attract media attention for a chess match between two Soviet players with similar-sounding names, but any flicker of interest from the outside world was snuffed out due to the sheer length the match (which lasted from early September, into Christmas, and six weeks into 1985).

Imagine if football were played this way, such that the finalists needed to win six games to decide the world cup winner, but practically every game finished in a draw, continuing for months and months. It would rightly provoke ridicule, turning to boredom as people stopped caring. That's why we have penalty shootouts.

After five months (!) and 48 games, Karpov held a five-wins-to-three lead (Kasparov was getting better as the match progressed, which is often attributed to him possessing superior stamina, being 11 years younger than Karpov). But the international federation had had enough and the match was abandoned with no result.

A rematch was held seven months later, which replaced first-to-six-wins with a new format, in which the title was awarded to the first player able to score 12 ½ points, over a maximum of 24 scheduled matches. All 24 games were required for Kasparov to wrest the title away, so in total it took 72 games of chess over more than 12 months to determine a winner between the two.

London Rules were an important innovation at the time but with the increased number of draws among modern-day grandmasters, it is difficult to see a return to the format any time soon.

Paris Opening

1. Nh3

In the Paris Opening, White's kingside knight hops from its starting square to the edge of the board where it is seriously misplaced. The opening is flamboyant, garish, and outlandish, much like the Parisians themselves.

The opening got its name thanks to one of Paris's resident amateurs, Charles Amar. In fact, **1. Nh3** is sometimes known as "The Amar Opening". Amar was not a particularly notable player but he was shrewd enough to play **1. Nh3** against an opponent who most certainly was – Savielly Tartakower. Tartakower was one of the highest profile grandmasters of the 1920s and 1930s, and although he never became the world champion, he always gave a good account of himself against the very best. Tartakower was most notable for his authorship and sharp wit. A few Tartakower-isms will give you a flavor of the man:

"The blunders are all there on the board, waiting to be made."

"No game was ever won by resigning."

"A game of chess has three phases: the opening, where you hope you stand better; the middlegame, where you think you stand better; and the ending, where you know you stand to lose."

Tartakower penned several famous books and contributed to widely circulated chess magazines. So, when Amar played **1. Nh3** against him while in Paris, Tartakower's wide reach was enough to make the name stick. Tartakower even adopted the move himself a few times. This story goes to show that there is more than one way to attain chess immortality. You don't need to become the best player in the world to get an opening named after you if you can discover an offbeat opening with no name yet and get someone more well-known to notice.

Paris has a far more central place in chess history than the opening that bears its name. The city was an intellectual hub during the Enlightenment; artists, musicians, and writers flocked there to be among one another and participate in the discourse. This new class of professional thinkers needed a meeting place and in Paris the place to be was the Café de la Régence.

The Régence was one of the famous coffee houses which had sprung up all over Europe from the 17th century onward. It has even been argued that the arrival of coffee was a contributing factor to the Enlightenment taking root in the first place. Instead of drinking themselves into a stupor with alcohol, people started to turn to mind-sharpening coffee.

The Régence became an important center for chess, hosting many strong tournaments of Europe's best players. Many of the central figures of the chess world played there at the height of its glory, including François-André Danican Philidor, Howard Staunton, Adolf Anderssen and Paul Morphy. Great philosophers and statesmen also frequented the venue, including Benjamin Franklin, Karl Marx, Napoleon Bonaparte and Voltaire.

Picture the scene in the Café de la Régence as coffee was supped, men smoked their pipes, ideas were exchanged and chess provided the entertainment for the casual players and the battleground for the serious ones. Divine.

By the time Charles Amar played **1. Nh3** in the early

20th century, the coffee houses were no longer hosting much chess. And because of him, Paris, one of the most significant cities in the history of chess, surrendered its name to one of the game's least important openings. *C'est la vie.*

Berlin Defense

1.	e4	e5
2.	Nf3	Nc6
3.	Bb5	Nf6

Berlin is the capital of Germany. The strong influence of German chess masters, and the seminal role Germany has played in chess history has resulted in a sprinkling of German words throughout the game. There is *zugzwang* (a situation where making <u>any</u> move will make a position worse, usually in the endgame), *zwischenzug* (an in-between move, often a check, to amplify the effect of the expected move, versus if that expected move had been played straight away) *blitz* (chess with a short time limit, usually five minutes per player or less), and of course, *patzer*, (a very weak player – from the German verb *patzen*, which in English means "to bungle").

The origin of the Berlin Defense comes from the first

comprehensive encyclopedia of chess, *Handbuch des Schachspiels* (English: "Handbook of Chess"), first published in Berlin in 1843. There, **3. ...Nf6** was recommended as a response to the Ruy López opening. Seven more editions were published over the next seven decades and it had grown to a 1,040-page behemoth by the time the eighth and final edition was completed in 1916. The *"Handbuch"* didn't fit in the hand anymore.

By playing **3. ...Nf6** in the Ruy López, Black lets White's light-squared bishop sit where it is and concentrates on his own piece development. Different variations of the Berlin Defense can be rich and tactical, but the opening is perhaps most notable for one of the lines where the queens come off the board early. This is the "Berlin Wall" variation, which carries a deserved drawish reputation.

One criticism of chess match play (one opponent against another for a set number of games, as is the format of modern world championship contests) is that the player with the lead will look to grind their way to victory by seeking draws and retain their advantage. The Berlin Wall has become a favorite weapon to achieve this.

In the 2014 world chess championship, after six games Magnus Carlsen held a two-wins-to-one lead over Vishy Anand. Carlsen wasn't about to take any risks; he played his next three games as White with the Berlin Wall to preserve his 1 point advantage. One game was a particular bore; a 20-move draw by repetition that both players knew by heart.

The drawn position on move 20: Carlsen vs. Anand, game 9 of 2014 world chess championship.

Carlsen got his desired two draws in game 7 and game 9, and won game 11 with Anand forced to do something risky with the twelfth and final game rapidly approaching. Alas, Anand couldn't tear down the Berlin Wall.

The Berlin Wall has its own historical significance as an impassable barrier. After the end of World War II, the Western allies and the Soviet Union partitioned Germany into West Germany and East Germany.

Berlin was located deep within the Soviet-controlled zone, but part of the pre-war capital was also awarded to the West.

The citizens of Berlin soon started to feel the stark differences between the two regimes: the western regions recovered relatively quickly, while East Berlin was continually beset by poverty and shortages. With life clearly better in the west, thousands of people in the eastern areas began emigrating. To put a stop to this, in 1961 the Berlin Wall was built by the East German government to stop their own people from escaping. When the wall was finally torn down in 1989, it was hugely symbolic – Germany soon became united again and the Soviet Union itself crumbled, ending the Cold War.

Vienna Game

1. e4   e5
2. Nc3

The Vienna Game looks rather non-threatening. Rather than use the second move to attack an enemy soldier with the more common **2. Nf3**, White defends one of its own pawns by playing **2. Nc3**. It is a fundamentally solid opening which can develop in many directions, both aggressive and quiet. One idea is to follow up with **3. f4** in the style of the King's Gambit (the "Vienna Attack"). Other lines see simple developing moves and the beginnings of a long-term positional game.

The Vienna Game received its name thanks to several strong Viennese players who worked on its development. Vienna was an important cultural center during the Enlightenment; Mozart played his music there and it held many strong chess tournaments. Wilhelm Steinitz – the first official world chess champion – gained one of his most important early victories by winning the Vienna City championship in 1861. Steinitz was also one of the opening's most ardent advocates.

The city of Vienna hosted the debut of a most extraordinary invention in 1770. Wolfgang von Kempelen claimed to have invented an automaton that could play a formidable game of chess against a human opponent. The machine consisted of a life-size model of a man in Ottoman robes, complete with moving arms and head. This figure sat at a cabinet with a large chess board on top and three doors at the front. The Austrian court assembled at Schönbrunn Palace to witness the machine's first game, and to the astonishment of all, this "Mechanical Turk" easily won. The Turk later traveled to the Café de la Régence in Paris and played against the world's best player, François-André Danican Philidor, as well as the prominent statesmen Napoleon Bonaparte and Benjamin Franklin.

If you hadn't guessed, it was a trick. Steam Age technology was not capable of the complex calculations required to play chess. The Turk concealed a strong chess-playing human operator inside the cabinet, who directed the moves to the model's arms via interior levers. Kempelen employed elaborate misdirection to prevent the secret from being discovered. The base of the machine contained dummy gears and cogs which appeared to be driving the operation. It also made a clockwork-like sound. The Turk survived inspection many times.

As interest in the Mechanical Turk grew, Kempelen became increasingly reluctant to expose his creation to further scrutiny. He would lie about it being under repair. He even completely dismantled The Turk until ordered by the Emperor to rebuild it. It may seem unbelievable to us that the Mechanical Turk was able to fool onlookers like this, but it was the early industrial revolution and all manner of new contraptions were hissing and spinning out hitherto impossible deeds. A chess-playing machine wouldn't have seemed completely out of the question to 18th century minds.

The first (real) chess-playing computer programs were not developed until the middle of the 20th century. Initially, the fact that computers could now play chess at all was remarkable enough, but these first programs could be defeated even by weak human players. However, the machines became better and better over the next few decades. They became able to evaluate millions of possible positions every second and began to pose a serious threat to even the best humans.

In the 1990s, the world's best player, Garry Kasparov, took on IBM's specially-built chess supercomputer *Deep Blue*. Under the spotlight of global media attention, the first six-game match in 1996 saw Kasparov defend the honor of humanity by triumphing with three wins, two draws and one loss. But in a rematch the following year, *Deep Blue* came out the victor – much to the upset of Kasparov.

Since that contest, chess programs have continued to get even stronger, while our brains seem much more confined to the limits of our biology. These days, a game between a professional grandmaster and freely available software running on an ordinary laptop computer would be an abject humiliation for the human. Having begun in Vienna as a hoax, the machines have finally prevailed.

Budapest Gambit

1.	d4	Nf6
2.	c4	e5

The name "Budapest" comes from the joining of two historic settlements on either side of the river Danube – Buda on the west, and Pest on the east. Today, cruise ships packed with tourists ply their way down the famous waterway taking in the beautiful bridges and gorgeous architecture of the Hungarian capital.

The first use of the Budapest Gambit at master level occurred in an 1896 game played in Budapest, won by a Hungarian native, Géza Maróczy. Normally a more defensive player, Maróczy was overtaken by a bout of aggression and lunged forward with his Black e-pawn. The move thus became named after the city in which it had been played.

The Budapest Gambit received additional attention after a Slovenian master named Milan Vidmar used it to beat Akiba Rubinstein in 1918. The story goes that Vidmar was despairing of his chances of beating Rubinstein and had no idea how to upset his opponent's legendary positional style. Vidmar asked a Hungarian friend what he should do, was given a crash course in the Budapest Gambit, and immediately used it to secure a famous victory.

These days, the Budapest Gambit has been declared "unsound", which means that when grandmasters play against other grandmasters, it should provide an advantage for White. Nevertheless, the Budapest Gambit is a fun way to play. We are often confronted with several possible moves which we adjudge to be roughly equal, but among these, there is frequently one move which leads to a far more interesting game. The Budapest Gambit is a reminder that when you play chess, you command the pieces. You don't need to play the objectively strongest move if you don't want to – you are free to settle for the more stimulating one if you wish.

Leningrad Variation

1.	d4	f5
2.	c4	Nf6
3.	g3	g6
4.	Bg2	Bg7
5.	Nf3	

Leningrad's historic and present name is St. Petersburg. When the communist revolution swept the Bolsheviks to power in 1917, the Russian seat of government was moved from St. Petersburg (called a third name, "Petrograd", at the time) to Moscow. The former capital was renamed Leningrad after the uprising's leader, Vladimir Lenin. Following the collapse of the USSR, a referendum saw the inhabitants decide to change the name back to St. Petersburg.

The Leningrad Variation of the Dutch Defense sees Black boldly march forward his kingside pawns.

Lenin himself was a keen chess player, and perhaps there are some faintly socialist undertones to this way of playing. Just look at how Black's kingside pawns support one another, like the idealized glorious proletariat.

The Leningrad Variation is so named because it was developed by players who came from there, particularly Boris Spassky, the tenth world chess champion. You may have noticed from reading other chapters in this book that Leningrad / St. Petersburg has been home to some of history's most significant chess players; besides Spassky, some of the other famous names to hail from there include Alexander Petrov, Semyon Alapin, Mikhail Chigorin, Mikhail Botvinnik and Viktor Korchnoi.

Chess had long been popular in Russia, but the Soviets laid the foundations for it to become a national matter of pride. They opened chess schools, subsidized training for promising young players, and promoted the game as a way of asserting the superiority of communism on the world stage. The efforts bore fruit as the Soviet Union held hegemony over the chess world championship from the start of the Cold War until the finish, save for one win by the American Bobby Fischer in 1972. Their players would even fix results against each other in tournament play to ensure a Soviet winner. Outsiders called it cheating, but subsuming the individual to the needs of the collective was a natural part of the ideology of the Soviet chess establishment.

Leningrad is famous for another reason in the history books – the tragic siege of the city in World War II, which lasted from September 1941 to January 1944. Over the 872-day siege, extensive bombardment and extreme famine caused the largest loss of life known in a modern city. Not even the atomic bombings of Hiroshima and Nagasaki killed as many people. But incredibly, the Leningrad chess championship was still played during the siege in 1941 (though not finished) and 1943.

Scheveningen Variation

1.	e4	c5
2.	Nf3	d6
3.	d4	cxd4
4.	Nxd4	Nf6
5.	Nc3	e6

Scheveningen is a seaside district of The Hague, which is the third-largest city in the Netherlands. The Hague is home to some of the world's most important international organizations, including the International Criminal Court, where war criminals are tried.

The Scheveningen Variation of the Sicilian Defense is characterized by Black having pawns on d6 and e6. Events at the 1923 Scheveningen chess tournament gave the variation its name. In one of the event's headline games, Géza Maróczy of Hungary was pitted against the Dutchman Max Euwe. Euwe, with the Black pieces, was convincingly defeated while playing what we now call the Scheveningen Variation – so convincingly that the whole setup lost popularity for many years. The chess world gave the variation the name of Scheveningen, almost as an obituary.

Advances in opening theory have given new respectability to the Scheveningen. Although White is ceded a space advantage, Black's position is very solid. Black also retains the ability to prepare a pawn break on d5 or e5 at an opportune moment.

"Scheveningen" is also the name that describes a system of chess match play between two teams, where every player in one team faces every player in the other team. This contrasts with the format of the bi-annual international chess olympiad, where teams nominate players for board one, board two and so on, and games only take place between the opposition players of the same board number.

The Scheveningen pairing system was named after that same 1923 chess tournament where 10 leading Dutch players faced 10 foreign masters. The Scheveningen format was also used in the 2002 contest between Russia and the Rest of the World, a contest of rapid games (25 minutes plus a 10 second increment), which resulted in a narrow win for the Rest of the World, 52 points to 48.

The Stories

This section groups together the rest. Some names given to chess openings are meaningful, some are playful – and some are just plain silly. While they don't merit a full chapter of their own, here are just a few of the more brassily-named ones, to give you a flavor:

The "Hippopotamus Defense" sees the Black player advance their pawns no further than the third rank and keeps all their other pieces behind them, like a dangerous hippo lurking under the calm of the water.

The "Monkey's Bum" was so named after a spectator saw it and exclaimed "If that works, then I'm a monkey's bum!" Bizarrely, the name stuck! Who says chess players don't have a sense of humor?

The "Halloween Gambit" is a shocking variation of the Four Knights Game. White ignores all common sense and gives up a knight for one of the center pawns that Black assumed was safely defended – a spooky move due to its sheer brazenness.

There are dozens, if not hundreds of other weird opening names like these. Some are known only inside a certain region, within a club or even nicknamed by just two players. For the openings that enjoy more of a widespread following, read on.

Dragon Variation

1.	e4	c5
2.	Nf3	d6
3.	d4	cxd4
4.	Nxd4	Nf6
5.	Nc3	g6

Dragons are mythical flame-snorting, flying beasts. They are frequently found in works of fantasy such as J.R.R. Tolkien's *The Hobbit* and George R.R. Martin's *A Song of Ice and Fire* series. The only tenuous connection between dragons and chess is the knight: dragons are slain by them, and chess has four of them on a board. Apart from that, dragons really have nothing whatsoever to do with chess.

The story of how the Dragon Variation got its name is tied to a Russian chess-playing astronomer: Fyodor Duz-Khotimirsky. He wrote: "I first uttered this name in Kiev, in 1901... While looking at the sky I noticed how the Dragon constellation resembled the [Black] pawn structure ...d6 ...e7... f7... g6... h7 seen in the Sicilian Defense. So, I decided to call the opening the Dragon Variation."

The Dragon Constellation (also known as *Draco*, which is the Latin word for "dragon") can be seen all year round in the Northern Hemisphere. According to Greco-Roman legend, Draco was a dragon at war with the gods. When the goddess of wisdom Minerva killed Draco, she threw it into the night sky where it remains.

This configuration of stars does indeed bear a resemblance to Black's pawn setup. But, dear reader, to say that the stars (or the pawns) look anything like a <u>dragon</u> is a stretch. But then, the same can be said about most star constellations. It takes a heck of an imagination to argue the tiny dots of light in the sky look like lions, bulls, fish – or dragons.

With Black's bishop coming to g7 to threaten White's center, the Dragon Variation is one of the game's most exciting, action-packed openings. After all, it would hardly do to give the name "dragon" to a timid opening. Duz-Khotimirsky was evidently quite pleased with the clever name he had invented, writing: "Of course the star system was itself named after a mythical dragon, so the association of the opening with the fire-breathing beast is fully appropriate."

Giuoco Piano

1. e4   e5
2. Nf3   Nc6
3. Bc4   Bc5

If you want to learn a new discipline, you must be prepared to experience failure. You fall off your first horse, you forget your first foreign language lesson, and you bang your fingers when you hammer your first nail. So too it is in chess. As soon as a new player has learned the moves, they will be taught humility very soon thereafter as others mercilessly exploit the frequent missteps.

But even if losing is what we expect when new to chess, we will feel a lot better if we can at least give a respectable account of ourselves. There is dignity to be found even in defeat if the struggle is well-fought. However, if we can't even last past the opening, there is only humiliation. Losing inside the first ten moves is the chess equivalent of a first-round knockout. You can't help but detect that subtle superior smirk from your opponent and you can't help but feel you didn't deserve to share the same board with them.

Such defeats for novices are most common in the sharper openings. There, they must navigate a veritable minefield and make correct move after correct move, lest their position explode out from under them. To avoid this, players new to chess will try to stick to openings where not too much can go too wrong, too quickly.

After **3. Bc4** (known as the "Italian Game"), if Black responds with **3. ...Bc5**, the opening is given an Italian name: *Giuoco Piano*, which literally means "quiet game". It is an opening that beginners gravitate towards because it reduces the possibility of rapid capitulation. Both sides follow the well-known opening maxims: develop pieces, occupy the center, and prepare to castle early. Neither player invites any immediate cut-and-thrust. If White's next move should be **4. d3**, a related opening name is bestowed, *Giuoco Pianissimo*, or "very quiet game".

The piano and the game of chess have much in common. Both require deep and serious study, both tend to attract introverts, and both have links with mathematics. Some rare fellows have even had the distinction of excelling at both disciplines. Mark Taimanov was among the world's top 20 chess players in the mid-20th century and was also a world-class concert pianist. Sergei Prokofiev, the Russian pianist, composer and conductor, managed to beat future world chess champion José Raúl Capablanca in a 1914 simul game.

Another thing shared by both chess and the piano is the linkage to the past. When sitting down to chess or to a piano, the same tools are in use as all the great masters who have come before you. New music is composed and new chess opening theory is advanced, but the 88 keys on a piano remain as they always have, as do the 32 pieces on a chess board.

Benoni Defense

1. d4   Nf6
2. c4   c5
3. d5

Ben-oni is a Hebrew term for "son of my sorrow" from the *Book of Genesis 35:18*. The Bible tells of a mother dying in childbirth and naming her baby "Benoni" before passing away. Slowly letting a winning position slip, touching a piece and then being obliged to move it, or badly messing up the opening can be enough to bring on the urge to cry out in despair. Nobody plays chess for any length of time without experiencing that sinking feeling, and for some of us it happens on a depressingly regular basis.

There are two versions of the origins of the Benoni Defense name. The definitive truth over which story is correct has unfortunately been lost to the annals of time, so below are both stories. Readers can decide for themselves which they prefer.

The more colorful version begins with a Jewish man named Aaron Reinganum. He was suffering from depression and the only thing that would cheer him up was chess. He wrote: "Whenever I felt in a sorrowful mood and wanted to take refuge from melancholy, I sat over a chessboard, for one or two hours according to circumstances."

Reinganum then went into a brooding period where he wrote a book about gambit defenses – an interesting way to try to recover from depression, to say the least. His book, *Ben-Oni oder die Vertheidigungen gegen die Gambitzüge im Schache* (English: Benoni, or Defenses Against the Gambits in Chess), started its title with "Ben-Oni" in tribute to his writing it during a time of deep sadness.

The other story is of a player (or players) named Benoni. This was the version Howard Staunton believed. A Spanish player named Ramón Rey Ardid supports this version of events, calling the opening "An old, audacious defense which comes from the English player Benoni". A Belgian grandmaster named Albéric O'Kelly de Galway wrote of two brothers named Benoni who lived in the 1830s.

The Benoni Defense splinters quickly into several

variations, each of which require precise play. There is the Old Benoni, the Czech Benoni, the Modern Benoni, and the Benko Gambit. Pawn breaks need to be monitored especially carefully, lest the opening infest you with the same sorrowful connotations of its name.

Grand Prix Attack

1. e4   c5
2. f4

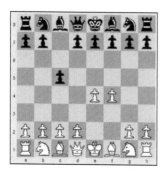

What do supercharged cars capable of speeds of over 200 miles per hour have in common with a board game where players can take half an hour (or even more) to contemplate a single move? In terms of the activities themselves: nothing. The Grand Prix Attack got its name from the scoring system that chess has occasionally borrowed from Formula 1 for season-long competitions.

To the average man on the street, motor racing is mostly interesting for just two reasons: when drivers overtake, and when they crash. There is not a lot of enjoyment for the audience when cars lead from pole position and defend their initial advantage throughout the whole race. Viewers want to see excitement, drama and swings in momentum.

Formula 1 racing tallies points from individual Grand Prix races to determine the overall season champion. The points are awarded to encourage the kind of racing the public want to see. As of the time of writing, each event on the Formula 1 calendar gave points according to the below scale:

Position	Points
1st	25
2nd	18
3rd	15
4th	12
5th	10
6th	8
7th	6
8th	4
9th	2
10th	1

This schedule incentivizes the drivers to take risks. Far more points are awarded for higher placings than minor placings, so a driver with ambitions of capturing the Formula 1 title must chase first and second places, even if it means flaming out completely on occasion in their pursuit.

White's move **2. f4** (or playing f4 early, on the third or fourth move) in response to the Sicilian Defense became known as the Grand Prix Attack due to its popularity in British weekend chess tournaments which used a scoring format with a similar philosophy.

An f4 pawn move in the Sicilian Defense likely avoids a lot of Black's opening preparation, but it's like a dangerous overtaking maneuver – the Grand Prix Attack will increase the likelihood of a win or a loss at the expense of a draw. But for the players trying to secure tournament wins rather than mid-table finishes, a better chance at capturing the full point is exactly what the Grand Prix Attack player is aiming for.

Orangutan Opening

1. b4

How did it come to pass that an intellectual game like chess ended up with an opening named after an ape? The story begins at a tournament held in 1924 in New York. It was attended by a veritable who's who of chess's elite including Lasker, Capablanca, Alekhine, Marshall, Réti, Maróczy and Tartakower.

One day, everybody gathered to visit the Bronx Zoo where they saw an orangutan. Most of the players simply admired it, but (as the story goes) Tartakower boldly asked the beast which move he should play the next day. Somehow, he got a reply from within the enclosure: **1. b4**.

Apparently convinced that he should favor the wisdom of a zoo animal over centuries of opening theory, the opinion of his peers, and his own better judgement, sure enough Tartakower played **1. b4** the next day in his game against Richard Réti. Incredibly, he even emerged from the opening with a superior position and eventually the game was drawn. It's an apocryphal tale, but an entertaining one nonetheless. The Orangutan Opening was born.

The 1920s were the heyday of the hypermodern openings. They were heady, highly experimental times when all kinds of new novelties were being discovered. Perhaps Tartakower thought he had found a genuine innovation. Or perhaps Susan the Orangutan really did communicate with him. Who knows.

The Orangutan Opening is also known by other names. The "Sokolsky Opening" is one, after a Soviet chess player and opening theoretician named Alexey Sokolsky, who wrote an entire book (!) about **1. b4** called *Debyut 1. b2-b4*. If it weren't for that book, Sokolsky would be long forgotten, though arguably obscurity is preferable to having one's memory for all time associated with a primate.

Another alternative name is the "Polish Opening" in tribute to Savielly Tartakower from Poland. The relative weakness of the move lends an extra humorous angle to the name "Polish Opening". You may have heard the Polish jokes that attribute useless inventions to them such as the solar-powered flashlight, submarine electric windows and the helicopter ejector seat. None of these inventions are real, by the way: they are just a way of making a good-natured dig at the Poles. Still, an opening like **1. b4** which doesn't offer much to White beyond shock value could very well be added to the list.

Toilet Variation

1. e4 c5
2. f4 d5
3. Nc3

The Toilet Variation was invented in a restroom by an unknown player. Nothing like the calm, serene isolation of a lavatory to generate inspiration! Unfortunately, experts believe the Toilet Variation will tend to see White get wiped out (pun intended).

Games of chess can last for hours, and players must be allowed to answer the call of nature. But the privacy of the toilet can be abused by unscrupulous players, particularly in the information age. The temptation to cheat in chess is very real. Prize money, careers and endorsements hang on the results achieved, just as they do in professional sports. Unlike anabolic steroids, cheating at chess will not show up in any urine samples, but the toilet can still be the scene of the crime. These days, the world's best humans can be crushed by software powered by a mobile phone. This means players could conceivably cheat in a critical position by visiting the toilet, sneaking a quick look at their phones to see what the computer recommends, memorizing the moves, and returning to the board.

In the 2006 world chess championship, Veselin Topalov complained about his opponent, Vladimir Kramnik, and his frequent visits to the bathroom. Kramnik vigorously denied any wrongdoing and explained that he simply preferred to drink a lot of water while playing chess – toilet breaks being the inevitable result.

The saga descended into farce. First, the organizers decided to institute a common bathroom. This upset Kramnik, and he forfeited a game in protest because the new bathroom was too small – he wanted to be able to walk around in it. The threat of the world chess championship being cancelled over something so petty eventually forced the resignation of the appeals committee. The new committee decided to reinstate the original, separate bathrooms.

No evidence of cheating was ever found in 2006, but a clear breach was uncovered in 2015. Gaioz Nigalidze was playing a game against an opponent named

Tigran Petrosian (confusingly, not <u>the</u> Tigran Petrosian, the world chess champion between 1963 and 1969. The man in this 2015 event had been given the same name by his chess-mad father and went on to become a grandmaster in his own right). After Petrosian became suspicious, the arbiters investigated the cubicle that Nigalidze had been repeatedly visiting and found a phone hidden behind some toilet paper. Nigalidze protested his innocence, but the phone was logged into an account in his name, with a chess application analyzing his game. You could say he was caught with his pants down. Nigalidze was expelled from the tournament and stripped of his grandmaster title.

Fried Liver Attack

1.	e4	e5
2.	Nf3	Nc6
3.	Bc4	Nf6
4.	Ng5	d5
5.	exd5	Nxd5
6.	Nxf7	Kxf7

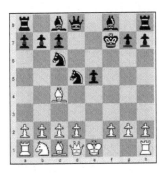

This book has described many openings as "sharp" and "aggressive", but none hold a candle to the exquisitely named Fried Liver Attack. White wastes no time on positional nonsense and instead throws the proverbial kitchen sink at his opponent by sacrificing a knight on move six. Black's king is drawn out into the open, which White hopes to exploit with a quick mating assault.

With its outlandish name, the Fried Liver Attack has no pretensions of being taken seriously. If Black keeps his cool, he can accept the gifted knight, parry off the attack, spend a move or two getting his king somewhere safer, and be satisfied with his material advantage. But it is easy to become alarmed when your opponent does something so bold, and that panic is exactly what White is counting on.

The temptation to try to win the game in the opening is alluring, especially to beginners. Those cursed with short attention spans may not enjoy the prospect of a long, drawn-out contest, and openings like the Fried Liver Attack at least offer the promise of a quick game (whether it results in a win or a loss). Springing a trap in the opening also promises to entirely avoid parts of the game at which a player has not yet become skilled. You don't need to know the ins and outs of middlegame strategic maneuvering or correct endgame play if you can deliver checkmate before most of the pieces have left the back rank.

Unfortunately, the siren song of quick wins can hold players back from improving. Sure, it might be possible to fool a few opponents, but at the cost of foregoing critical practice of positions later in the game. If you have a shortcoming, the thing to do - if you want to get better - is to expose yourself to it as often as possible. That said, it is undeniable that a swift conquest can still be pleasurable. Treat yourself from time to time, so long as you don't <u>always</u> try to win through such cheap tricks at the expense of in-depth study.

The Fried Liver Attack arises from White's first three moves being played along the lines of the Giuoco Piano opening (a name with Italian origins). The Italian connection continues, as the Fried Liver Attack got its name from the Italian way of preparing liver, known as *Fegatello*. A pig's liver is cut, crushed and wrapped in a net, then roasted over an open flame or in a skillet. The metaphor is Black's king: it is drawn out into the open so that White can turn up the heat. One slip and Black may find his precious monarch cooked. It is also an Italian idiom to say that something is "dead as a piece of liver".

If you like heated openings, and don't mind sacrificing a piece so you can immediately begin a king hunt, consider adding the Fried Liver Attack to the menu.

Before You Go...

Now that you have learned the stories behind the opening names, hopefully you are even more inspired to learn how to play them!

www.chessopeningnames.com is host to dozens of comprehensive video training courses taught by the world's best chess teachers. Watch your rating skyrocket as you crush your opponents, and then rub it in with the superior knowledge of the opening names that you have gleaned from reading this book.

I would love to hear your feedback on *Chess Opening Names*. Please visit www.chessopeningnames.com and request the stories behind more opening names. I will be sure to add the most popular requests to the website and to future editions of this book.

Finally, a reminder. There are several free bonuses for readers of *Chess Opening Names* to download:

- A pgn file of all the openings and variations named in this book, so you can play through and practice them on your computer.
- A family tree index of all the moves named in this book – for example, which moves are branches of the "core" openings, and the points at which the different names diverge.

- A video explanation of how algebraic chess notation works – if you didn't understand the meaning of the script used throughout the book such as **1. e4 e5**, this video will teach you.
- Sample chapters of my other books.

To download these free bonuses, head to www.chessopeningnames.com, scroll to the "Bonus Content" section and use your email address to subscribe.

Thank you for reading!

Acknowledgments

I was the fortunate recipient of a generous amount of invaluable input from early readers. My sincere thanks go to Oliver Hornbrook, Ian Sellen, Sue Rose, Mike Asplet, Richard Fireman, Ken Pow, Adrian Saw, Philip Rossiter, Eric Holcomb, Ryan Schwiebert, Michael Sole, Kirsti Rawstron, Kasper van der Meulen, Nicolas Bosma, Gabriela Dunowska, Bill Feldman, Bob Schleppi, Andrew Stone, Stephen Pride and Gregory Krog Jr. It is no exaggeration to say that your helpful remarks have improved *Chess Opening Names* several-fold.

I grew up in Wellington, New Zealand. It's where I learned chess and where I still enjoy returning to when my schedule allows. Wellington is a far outpost of the chess world, yet whether you are completely new to the game, hold an official master title, or are somewhere in between, Wellington can provide you with a welcoming environment and healthy competition. I hugely appreciate those Wellingtonian players that I have faced over the years – for the contests we have fought, but more importantly, for the friendship. When it became known that I was writing this book, Wellingtonian players always said the right words to encourage me to continue.

Tbilisi, Georgia has been my more recent home. When I tell people that I am living in "Georgia", most assume that I must mean the American state of Georgia, the capital of which is Atlanta. But no – the nation of Georgia is a small, charming country nestled on the shore of the Black Sea, at the foot of the Caucasus Mountains. It has breathtaking natural beauty, excellent wine, and an old-world charm unlike anywhere else I have yet encountered. Vera Park in central Tbilisi is the place where a clutch of old men happily play chess all day long. Though none of these gents are fluent in English, I still want to express my gratitude here for the warm welcome I was guaranteed anytime I felt like a game as I wrote this book. მადლობა!

Credit goes to Bill Forster and his "Tarrasch" graphic user interface software for the diagrams that appear throughout. The excellent program includes a comprehensive opening database, a powerful computer engine and allows users the ability to intuitively add annotations and different move variations. Head to www.triplehappy.com to download the software for yourself for free.

Special thanks to the man I consider the world's foremost chess instructor. To grandmaster Simon Williams (the "Ginger GM"), you have a real gift for making chess enjoyable for your fans. I am thrilled that you agreed to write the foreword for this book, and for the typically entertaining style you wrote it in.

Finally, a dedication to my father, Kim Rose. He taught me how to play chess as a child and sparked my interest in the game. To this day we are still rather evenly matched and I look forward to many more enthralling battles with him in years to come.

Sources

Benko, P. *The Benko Gambit* (1974)

Corfield, J. *Pawns in a Greater Game: The Buenos Aires Chess Olympiad August – September 1939* (Corfield and Company, 2015)

de Firmian, N. *Batsford's Modern Chess Openings* – 15th Edition (Batsford, 2009)

Fox, M. & James, R. *The Even More Complete Chess Addict* – Revised Edition (Faber and Faber, 1993)

Golombek, H. *Réti's Best Games Of Chess* (1954)

Harper, W. & Anderson, L. "*Life And Chess*" YouTube video lecture series (2015–2017)

Hooper, D. & Whyld, K. *The Oxford Companion To Chess* – 2nd Edition (Oxford University Press, 1992)

Katz, G., Maguire T. & Zwick, E. (producers) *Pawn Sacrifice* (film) (Distributed by Bleecker Street, 2014)

Kasparov G. with Greengard, M. *How Life Imitates Chess* (William Heinemann, 2007)

Keene, R. *Aron Nimzowitsch: A Reappraisal* (1974)

Lawson, D. edited by Aiello, T. *Paul Morphy: The Pride And Sorrow Of Chess* - New Edition (University of Louisiana at Lafayette Press, 2010)

Neishtadt, I. translated by Neat, K. *Play the Catalan* (Pergamon Press, 1987–1988)

Reshevsky, S. *Great Chess Upsets* (Arco Publishing, 1976)

Shenk, D. *The Immortal Game: A History Of Chess Or How 32 Carved Pieces On A Board Illuminated Our Understanding of War, Art, Science and the Human Brain* (Anchor Books, 2006)

Standage, T. *The Mechanical Turk: The True Story Of The Chess-Playing Machine That Fooled The World*, (Allen Lane, 2002)

van der Sterren, P. *FCO: Fundamental Chess Openings* (Gambit Publications, 2009)

Various articles appearing in chess.com, chesscafe.com, chessgames.com, chesshistory.com, wikipedia.com, Chess Life Magazine, and New In Chess Magazine.

Alphabetical Index of Names

63480429R00129

Made in the USA
San Bernardino, CA
19 December 2017